Charles Baudelaire Revisited

Twayne's World Authors Series
French Literature

David O'Connell, Editor
Georgia State University

TWAS 827

CHARLES BAUDELAIRE
Photograph by Carjat

Charles Baudelaire Revisited

Lois Boe Hyslop

The Pennsylvania State University

Twayne Publishers • New York
Maxwell Macmillan Canada • Toronto
Maxwell Macmillan International • New York Oxford Singapore Sydney

Charles Baudelaire Revisited
Lois Boe Hyslop

Twayne Publishers
Macmillan Publishing Company
866 Third Avenue
New York, New York 10022

Maxwell Macmillan Canada, Inc.
1200 Eglinton Avenue East
Suite 200
Don Mills, Ontario M3C 3N1

Macmillan Publishing Company is part of the Maxwell Communication Group of
Companies.

Library of Congress Cataloging-in-Publication Data

Hyslop, Lois Boe, 1908-.
    Chalres Baudelaire revisited / Lois Boe Hyslop.
        p.   cm. — (Twayne's world authors series ; TWAS 827. French
    literature)
    Includes bibliographical references and index.
    ISBN 0-8057-8265-6
    1. Baudelaire, Charles, 1821–1867—Criticism and interpretation.
I. Title.   II. Series: Twayne's world authors series ; TWAS 827.
III. Series: Twayne's world authors series. French literature.
PQ2191.Z5H93   1992
841'.8—dc20   91-34028
                                                           CIP

The paper used in this publication meets the minimum requirements
of American National Standard for Information Sciences—Permanence
of Paper for Printed Library Materials. ANSI Z3948-1984. ∞™

10 9 8 7 6 5 4 3 2 1

Printed in the United States of America

Contents

Preface

Few modern writers have had as much written about them as Charles Baudelaire or have been as universally admired by readers and critics alike. Perhaps even fewer have had their works read as avidly and enthusiastically almost everywhere throughout the world. In fact, Paul Valéry once wrote that it was only with Baudelaire that French poetry went beyond the frontiers of France. The distinguished Baudelairean scholar, the late W. T. Bandy, went even further and proved conclusively that no modern poet has been translated in as many languages and in as many different countries.

In Baudelaire's own day only a few—Flaubert, Gautier, and De Vigny among them—recognized the originality and strange beauty of Baudelaire's verse and the astute perception of his criticism. Yet as Dumesnil notes—and not without a certain amount of exaggeration—one need read only 20 lines of *Les Fleurs du mal, L'Art romantique,* or *Curiosités Esthétiques* to discover the genius of the poet and the lucid judgment of a great writer who was among the first to recognize the rare gift of Delacroix, of Manet, and of Wagner. It is true that Baudelaire's deliberate attempts to shock and surprise did much to attract unfavorable criticism and to conceal his real genius. There is no doubt that his tragic existence was in no small part the result of his own making. He could be difficult, irascible, and almost childish at times when thwarted in his plans or unable to gain his own way.

At other times he could be kindness itself, as with the mentally unbalanced Méryon or the sensitive and excessively shy Charles Barbara, the rather mediocre writer who, as Charles Asselineau has told us, Baudelaire "adopted because of his restive, obstinate temperament, and whom he loved for his perseverance and for his honest hard work." In fact, the devoted friendship of so fine a person as the "gentle Asselineau" is alone testimony of the goodness that so often lay buried and unrecognized in Baudelaire's heart.

Unlike Hugo, Balzac, and Delacroix, Baudelaire was never able to know the admiration of his contemporaries or to enjoy the comforts of a prosperous existence. Nor was he to achieve the serenity that results from a life well lived and from a task well done. Haunted by debts, disease, and the fear of insanity or of approaching death, he transformed the passions and emotions of his tortured soul into the beauty of verse and gave the age a new poetic style in which is to be found a mixture of the base with the sublime. Baudelaire, Eric Auerbach has wisely noted, could not hide behind his work, but is to be found right in the middle of it. His art, he maintains, is built from the process of his own destruction. The careful reader will not fail to note the beauty and mystery of modern urban life in his prose poems, as well as the relentless struggle, particularly in his poetry, of the aesthetic pleasures of life in conflict with the psychological and moral anguish of guilt that so often accompanied those very pleasures.

I would like to thank James A. Jamison for the encouragement and invaluable aid he has lent me in the preparation and completion of this book.

Chronology

1821   Charles Baudelaire born 9 April in Paris.

1827   François Baudelaire, Charles's father, dies at age of 68. (Charles's mother, Caroline Archembaut Defayis, is 34 years younger than her husband.)

1828   Caroline Baudelaire marries Major (later General) Aupick 8 November.

1832   Charles and his mother go to Lyons, where his stepfather had been sent to repress the uprisings and where he attends the Collège royal.

1836   Returns with family to Paris. Attends the Lycée Louis-le-Grand.

1839–1840   Takes a room in the Pension Bailly. Leads a care-free life in the Latin Quarter. Contracts a venereal disease in the autumn of 1839.

1841   Alarmed by the Bohemian life of Charles, his family sends him on a sea voyage. He embarks on the *Paquebot-des-Mers-du-Sud* on 9 June, planning to sail to Calcutta, but goes only as far as the islands of Mauritius and Réunion.

1842   Returns to France on the *Alcide* 18 February. On turning 21 inherits 100,000 gold francs left him by his father. Moves to the Ile St-Louis where for a time he lives in the Hôtel Pimodan (Hôtel de Lauzun). Becomes a close friend of the painter Emile Deroy.

1844   To prevent Charles from squandering his inheritance, Mme Aupick arranges the appointment of a legal guardian, M. Narcisse-Désiré Ancelle, who was to have complete control over the remaining capital and pay Charles the interest in monthly installments.

1845   *Le Salon de 1845* published in May. Baudelaire makes a feeble suicide attempt 30 June.

1846   "Le Musée classique du bazar Bonne-Nouvelle" published in *Le Corsaire-Satan* 21 January.

1847   Publishes the short novel *La Fanfarlo* in January. Interest in Edgar Allan Poe is aroused by his reading of Isabelle Meunier's translation of *The Black Cat* in *La Démocratie pacifique*.

1848   Takes a small part in the Revolution of 1848. Jules Buisson claims to have seen Baudelaire brandishing a new rifle and shouting, "We must go and shoot General Aupick." With Champfleury and Toubin publishes two issues of the newspaper *Le Salut public*, 27 February, 1 and 2 March. Is associated with *La Tribune nationale*, a moderate socialist newspaper. Takes a small part in the June insurrection. Writes his first letter to Proudhon, 21 August. In October serves as editor in chief of the Châteauroux newspaper *Le Représentant de l'Indre*.

1851   "Du Vin et du hachisch" published in *Le Messager de l'assemblée*, 7, 8, 11, 12 March. Eleven poems published in *Le Messager de l'assemblée*, 9 April. Shows Asselineau a calligraphed manuscript of his poems in September. "Les Drames et les Romans honnêtes" published in the *Semaine théâtrale*, 27 November. Baudelaire is disillusioned by the coup d'état of Louis Napoleon, 2 December.

1852   "L'Ecole païenne" published in the *Semaine théâtrale*, 22 January. "Edgar Allan Poe, sa vie et ses ouvrages" published in *La Revue de Paris* in March and April.

1855   Publishes a series of articles on the World's Fair held in Paris, including articles on Eugène Delacroix and Jean Auguste Ingres. "De l'Essence du rire et généralement du comique dans les arts plastiques" published in *Le Portefeuille*, 8 July.

1856   Publishes *Histoires extraordinaires*, the first volume of Baudelaire's translations of Poe's stories, 12 March.

1857   Publishes *Nouvelles Histoires extraordinaires*, the second volume of his translations of Poe, 8 March. First edition of *Les Fleurs du mal* published on 25 June. On 20 August, the court orders six poems of *Les Fleurs du mal* to be removed from the volume. Publishes *Quelques caricaturistes français*, 1 October, and *Quelques caricaturistes étrangers*, 15 October.

1858   Publishes a translation from Poe, *Aventures d'Arthur Gordon*

Pym, 13 May. "De l'Idéal artificiel—Le Hachisch" published in the *Revue contemporaine,* 30 September.

1859   *Le Salon de 1859* appears in serial form, 10 and 20 June, 1 and 20 July. Publishes *Théophile Gautier,* a pamphlet with a letter-preface by Victor Hugo, 26 November.

1860   Publishes *Les Paradis artificiels* in May.

1861   In February second edition of *Les Fleurs du mal* published with 35 new poems. *Richard Wagner et "Tannhäuser" à Paris.* From 15 June to 15 August nine of the ten critical essays constituting "Réflexions sur quelques-uns de mes contemporains" published in the *Revue fantaisiste.*

1862   On 2 August seven critical essays on Hugo, Desbordes-Valmore, Gautier, Banville, Dupont, Leconte de Lisle, Le Vavasseur and seven poems appear in Eugène Crépet's anthology *Les Poètes français.*

1863   "L'Oeuvre et la vie d'Eugène Delacroix" published in *L'Opinion nationale,* 2 September, 14 and 22 November. Translation of Poe's *Eureka* published in November. "Le Peintre de la vie moderne" published in *Le Figaro,* 26 and 29 November, 3 December.

1864   Arrives in Brussels 24 April to give a series of lectures and to find a publisher for his collected works.

1865   *Histoires grotesques et sérieuses,* the fifth and final volume of Poe translations, published 16 March.

1866   Suffers a slight stroke in March while visiting the church of Saint-Loup in Namur. Later his condition worsens and he becomes partially paralyzed and aphasic. Is brought back to Paris on 2 July and enters the nursing home of Doctor Duval. *Les Épaves de Charles Baudelaire* is published.

1867   Dies 31 August; buried at the Montparnasse cemetery 2 September.

Chapter One

The Man

Early Years

"Even as a child I felt in my heart two opposite emotions: the horror of life and the ecstacy of life," Baudelaire writes in that part of his *Journaux intimes* (*Intimate Journals*) known as *Mon Coeur mis à nu* (*My Heart Laid Bare*).[1] Elsewhere in his autobiographical notes he speaks of the "loneliness" and "solitude" that were "the constant companions" of his life, despite a "very keen taste for life and pleasure" (*OC,* 1:680).[2] His confession does much to explain both the life and works of one who was to become not only a remarkable critic but also one of the world's greatest poets.

Charles Baudelaire was born in Paris on 9 April 1821 to 28-year-old Caroline Archenbaut Defayis (sometimes written Dufäys or Dufays) and 62-year-old Joseph-François Baudelaire. Caroline, was born in exile in London in 1793 and was brought up in Paris, after the death of her parents, in the family of an old friend of her father. Penniless but attractive and charming, she married Baudelaire, a courtly, white-haired widower with a comfortable fortune, when she was 26.

As a young man, François-Joseph studied philosophy and theology at the University of Paris and was ordained a priest at the end of 1783 or 1784. A member of the Chalons diocese, known for its strong Jansenist leanings, he served for a time as assistant master at the Collège de Sainte-Barbe. Later he became a tutor to the sons of the duc de Choiseul-Praslin, at whose home he came to know the philosopher Marquis de Condorcet and the physiologist Cabinis. An amateur painter with little or no real talent, he also associated with the artists of his generation—among them Guillaume Regnaut, Pierre-Paul Prud'hon, and Naigeons, and the sculptor Ramey. Years later (30 December 1857), after discovering in a dealer's shop some paintings done by his father, Baudelaire wrote his mother recounting the incident and lamenting that he had no money, "not even enough to make a deposit. My father was a wretched artist," he added, "but all these old things have a moral value."[3]

Like many of his fellow priests, François-Joseph renounced the priesthood during the Revolution, and in 1797 married Rosalie Janin, who died a few years later in 1814, leaving a son, Claude-Alphonse. It was also during the Revolution that François-Joseph was able to aid his former benefactors, the Choiseul-Praslins, who, some years later, after regaining their position and influence, were to show their gratitude by obtaining for him a profitable position in the administration of the Senate.

The marriage of Caroline and François Baudelaire was to last only a few years. On 10 February 1827, François Baudelaire died, leaving his young widow to care for their sensitive, precocious child. Though only six, Charles was never to forget his father's affection, courtesy, and elegant eighteenth-century manners. On their long walks in the Luxembourg Gardens, the distinguished old gentleman would talk seriously to his young son, pointing out to him the beauties of art and architecture. It was undoubtedly such memories that helped to shape the manners of the future poet—particularly the extreme politeness thought by many to be mere affectation—and to encourage his taste for the visual arts, which were later to become for him a consuming passion.

After his father's death, Charles became closer to his mother, whom he adored and whose love he had no wish to share. The summer days spent together in their small house in Neuilly became for him an "innocent paradise" he was later to recall in a short, untitled poem in *Les Fleurs du mal*. Twenty months later his childhood paradise was destroyed when his mother married the 40-year-old Major Jacques Aupick, a brilliant career officer who was to become a general, an ambassador, and finally a senator. Although Charles must have resented the man who put an end to his idyllic happiness, it was not until some years later that he revealed his bitter antipathy. When, in November 1831, Aupick (now lieutenant-colonel) was sent to Lyons to quell the riots, he enrolled his stepson as a boarder at the Collège royal there; the pampered 10-year-old lived a strict life not unlike that of a barracks.

Promoted to the rank of colonel and recalled to Paris in 1836, Aupick placed Charles, then 15, in the famous Lycée Louis-le-Grand where, during the first year of his stay, he had a creditable record. While there he began reading Romantic literature with avid interest, confiding to his mother his special admiration for Hugo's dramas and poetry and for Charles-Augustin Sainte-Beuve's novel *Volupté*. For the melodramas of Eugène Sue he had only scorn.

At Louis-le-Grand the young Charles seemed to undergo a change. His polite insolence to his professors and his insubordination became more and more noticeable so that, as a result of some trifling incident, he was dismissed from school in 1839. To prepare him for his *baccalauréat,* his parents sent him as a boarder to a M. Lasègue who prepared him for his examinations, which he successfully passed in August 1839. Once Charles had become a *bachelier,* his parents hoped he would choose a career in the diplomatic service. Charles, however, refused and, to their consternation, announced his intention of becoming a writer. From that time on, Charles was in open revolt against his stepfather, although in earlier years he had shown him no animosity. When he was 17 he had even accompanied him on a holiday trip to the Pyrenees, during which he is said to have written the poem "Incompatibilité."

To keep peace in the family, Charles agreed to prepare for his entrance examinations for the Ecole des Chartes. Living in the Pension Bailly, a well-known student lodging house, he became a member of the "Norman School" founded by his good friend Gustave Le Vavasseur and made up of amateur poets among his classmates who were greatly influenced by the Romantic School, especially Sainte-Beuve and Gautier.

Even more important, lacking any real supervision, Baudelaire plunged into the Bohemian life of the Latin Quarter. To the surprise of his companions, the impeccably dressed dandy chose for his mistress a small, ugly prostitute by the name of Sarah, whose squint-eyed appearance inspired Charles to call her Louchette. From her he contracted the venereal disease that was eventually to destroy his health and to hasten his death. In *Les Fleurs du mal* Baudelaire alludes in a titleless sonnet to the sordid affair: "One night when, near a frightful Jewess, lying/Like one corpse outstretched beside another." That Baudelaire was deeply disturbed by the illness that he had contacted is readily apparent in the sardonic epitaph which he wrote for himself about this time: "Here lies one who, having too much loved a filthy broad,/Still young was laid away beneath the sod."

Disturbed by their son's conduct, M. and Mme Aupick decided to take five thousand francs from Charles's inheritance and send him on a trip to India, hoping that a break with his associates would prove beneficial. On 9 June 1841, Charles sailed from Bordeaux on a ship called *Paquebot-des-Mers-du-Sud (Southern Seas).* Nine months later he was back in Paris, entertaining his friends with highly imaginative tales of his adventures. From the scrupulous account kept by Captain Saliz of *Paquebot-des-Mers-du-Sud,* in whose care the young man had been placed, we learn that, contrary to his claims, Charles had never reached India; his homesickness and growing melancholy had so alarmed the captain that he decided to send his charge back to France. After a violent storm (during which, according to Saliz, Baudelaire remained surprisingly brave among the frightened passengers) the ship cast anchor on the island of Mauritius. There Charles made the ac-

quaintance of M. Autard de Bragard and his charming and attractive young
wife, in whose company he found much pleasure and understanding. Waiting for a return boat to France at the Ile Bourbon, Baudelaire remained on
board—or so, at least, he claimed—and wrote a charming though somewhat conventional sonnet, "A une Créole," which he dedicated to Mme
Autard and enclosed in a gracious letter to her husband. Published in
l'Artiste in 1845, it was to be the first poem appearing under Baudelaire's
signature.

Though Charles never reached India, the trip left an indelible mark on
his poetry and furnished him with a store of images he was to draw on
throughout his life. It was also to inspire "The Albatross," "Very Far from
Here," and "To a Malabar Girl," poems published and undoubtedly
written—at least in final form—a number of years later.

The Young Dandy and the Black Venus

On his return to Paris, Charles renewed his friendship with his friends
from the Pension Bailly—Ernest Prarond, Louis-Gustave Le Vavasseur,
Philippe de Chenevières, Dozon, and Jules Buisson. Budding young poets,
they invited Baudelaire to join them in publishing a book of verse at their
own expense. Though Le Vavasseur maintained that Baudelaire withdrew
his poems in response to some critical remarks made by his coauthors, some
years later Prarond admitted that a few of the unsigned poems were really
those of the future poet.

In April 1842, Charles reached his majority and came into possession of
the hundred thousand francs left him in his father's will. To escape M.
Aupick's critical eye, Charles had already left home and was living on the Ile
Saint-Louis. With his newly acquired fortune he was able to move in 1843
from his simple lodgings to the Hôtel Pimodan (Lauzun), a beautiful man-
sion, built by a rich nobleman in the seventeenth century, that had been
converted into apartments. There he was a neighbor of the artist Ferdinand
Boissart, in whose lavish apartment, containing among other things a piano
painted by Watteau, he met Théophile Gautier and occasionally attended
the meetings of the Hashish Club.

To furnish his own small apartment under the eaves, Baudelaire bought
furniture and paintings at exorbitant prices from Arondel, an unscrupulous
dealer, who had his shop on the first floor of the Pimodan. The promissory
notes that Baudelaire signed in lieu of payment were to haunt him all his
life. At the time of his death he was still bravely struggling to pay off his
many debts. It was also at this time that Baudelaire became known as a

dandy; his extravagant and striking costumes were only to add to his debts and attract attention to his person.

In the spring of 1842, Baudelaire made the acquaintance of Jeanne Duval, also known as Lemer or Prosper, who was referred to by the poet's indignant mother as the "Black Venus." A striking quadroon, she was to have a greater influence on him than any other woman; some of his finest poems were filled with references to her dark beauty, the perfume of her blue-black hair, the sinuous grace of her movements. In his letters and his journal *Mon Coeur mis à nu,* he speaks of her first with passion and gratitude, then with anger and disgust, and finally with pity and remorse.

Jeanne remains a somewhat mysterious figure; she came into Baudelaire's life in 1842 and quietly disappeared after his death in 1867. At the time he met her, she was a third-rate actress in a cheap theater of the Latin Quarter. After she became his mistress, Baudelaire installed her for a short time in a small apartment on the Ile Saint-Louis, where the exotic beauty he attributed to her in his verse was set off by Eastern rugs and hangings.

In the meantime Baudelaire's parents had become alarmed at his prodigality and decided it was necessary to intervene. When it was discovered that he had already spent almost half his inheritance in the course of only two years, they decided to place him under the legal guardianship of Narcisse-Désiré Ancelle, a conscientious middle-class lawyer of Neuilly, whose good but bungling intentions were long misunderstood by his ward. Baudelaire's frequent requests for loans or advances on his monthly allowance were usually refused by Ancelle, who thought only of the young man's future welfare. As a result Charles was often obliged to turn to his mother for financial assistance. Although at times Charles was almost beside himself with rage and despair, his protests were ignored, and he was forced to endure all his life the humiliation of living under a legal guardianship. It was only in his last unhappy years that Baudelaire finally came to appreciate the kindly intentions of the old gentleman who despite everything had grown sincerely fond of his irascible ward.

Until this time Baudelaire had published almost nothing. He had collaborated in composing *Les Mystères galans des théâtres de Paris* (*Amatory Mysteries of the Theaters of Paris*) and had written a few reviews for minor Paris newspapers. Meanwhile he had earned a reputation for eccentricity and even immorality. He was a brilliant conversationalist and would spend evenings with his friends telling stories that were as improbable as they were sensational. Like many artists and writers of his day, he enjoyed shocking more conservative members of society; in this way he did much to create the

legend that still surrounds his name. At the same time, he enjoyed more serious conversation about art and literature.

Baudelaire in 1845

It was in 1845 that Baudelaire published his first important work, *Le
Salon de 1845*. It was no accident that he began his literary career as an art
critic. Ever since his childhood, painting had been his chief passion: "to glorify the cult of images (my great, my only, my earliest passion)," he wrote in
Mon Coeur mis à nu (*OC,* 1:701). And throughout his entire life this attraction never lessened. His interest had first been aroused by his father; later, at
the Pension Bailly, he paid almost daily visits to the Louvre; at the Hôtel
Pimodan he cultivated the acquaintance of the artist Fernand Boissard; and
finally, after moving to the Ile St-Louis, a haven for a small colony of artists,
he had an even greater opportunity to talk with various artists and to ob-
serve them at their work.

Of the many artists he met there none influenced him more than Emile
Deroy (1820–46), an impoverished young man who died tragically, alone
and friendless, soon after leaving the Ile St-Louis. The two became inseparable friends, visiting studios, museums, and cafés together. From Deroy
Baudelaire obviously learned much about the technical problems of painting; it is no accident that in the *Salon de 1845* the author is more concerned
with the problem of technique than in any other essay. Deroy was especially
fascinated with the problem of color. Théodore de Banville, at whose apartment Baudelaire, Deroy, and the poet songwriter Pierre Dupont often used
to meet, recalls how the artist would spend the evening seeking unusual
color harmonies by working with bits of colored material attached to a piece
of string.[4]

It was at the Salon of 1845 that Deroy introduced Baudelaire to
Asselineau, a writer, bibliophile, and, during the last years of his life, the di-
rector of the Bibliothèque Mazarine. With his fine, sensitive mind, critical
judgment, and self-effacing nature, the "gentle Asselineau" came to know
and appreciate the genius of Baudelaire better than any of his other friends.
He was to stand by the poet in his last illness and, with Banville, edited the
posthumous edition of Baudelaire's works in 1868. He also published a
moving biography of the unhappy poet in the following year.

The three friends visited the Salon together and would go from the Louvre to a tavern on the rue Carrousel to draw up a list of the painters
Baudelaire and Asselineau planned to discuss. Not too surprisingly, the re-

views of the two critics were in complete agreement, although due to space restrictions Asselineau's referred to fewer paintings than Baudelaire's.

Among the works left by Deroy is the famous portrait of Baudelaire as a young dandy, now hanging in the museum of Versailles. In it, Baudelaire is dressed all in black, only a touch of white showing in the neckline and at the cuffs. Handsome with his long silky hair and beard, the poet is shown seated in an armchair, one hand supporting his head while the other grasps the arm of the chair. The intensity of his gaze and the almost contorted position of his hands add a strange quality to the pose. The portrait was rejected by the Salon of 1846, which added to Deroy's bitterness and contributed to his suicide.

Among Deroy's best works is *La Mendiante rouge,* the portrait of an auburn-haired young street singer who was a familiar figure in the streets and cafés that Baudelaire and his friends frequented. Evidently Baudelaire and the poet Théodore de Banville also decided to celebrate the same young girl in verse, Baudelaire with "A une Mendiante rousse" ("To a Red-haired Beggar Girl"), and Banville with "A une petite Chanteuse des Rues" ("To a Little Street-singer").

Although Baudelaire's *Salon de 1845* attracted a certain amount of attention, it did not meet with the success that its author had hoped. Harassed by debts and the financial restrictions imposed by Ancelle, overwhelmed by the difficulty of earning a living by his pen, Baudelaire fell deeper and deeper into depression until he made a half-hearted attempt at suicide by inflicting on himself a slight knife wound. In his letter, which Jeanne took to his mother, he explained his state of mind and asked that his money be left to Jeanne, in whom alone he had "found any peace"—a thinly veiled criticism directed at his mother.

Whether or not Baudelaire's attempt to commit suicide was a hoax concocted to reconcile him with his parents or a sincere act on his part remains a moot question. The fact that he later joked about it with his friends may simply have been an attempt to hide his unhappiness and his true feelings. Throughout his life he invented monstrous lies about himself in an effort to conceal his hurt pride. It is certainly true that the suicide attempt and the letter itself were, at least in part, an effort to rebuke his mother who he felt had rejected him: "She has her *husband* . . . I have only *Jeanne Lemer,*" he wrote to Ancelle (*Corr.,* 1:125). Whatever the case, a temporary reconciliation was effected. Charles returned home only to take his departure after a stay of a few months, leaving a note for his mother in which he attributed his decision to his stepfather's critical attitude.

A New Beginning

After leaving his family for the second time, Baudelaire took a room at the Hôtel de Dunkerque, 32 rue Lafitte, and attempted to renew his literary activities. On 24 November 1845 he published an unsigned satiric article, "Comment on paie ses dettes quand on a du génie" ("How a Genius Pays His Debts"), in which he lampooned Balzac's use of ghostwriters. The fact that Baudelaire attacked the famous author of *La Comédie humaine,* for whom he had always had the greatest admiration, is surprising, especially since he too would prostitute his art in an effort to pay his debts. Only a few months later, in February 1846, Baudelaire published a long short story, "Le Jeune Enchanteur," which in 1950 was discovered by W. T. Bandy to be a translation of "The Young Enchanter," an anonymous story from an English keepsake volume. Bandy's careful investigation has shown the author to be the Reverend George Croly, an English divine who hid his secular literary achievements in anonymity.[5] When Baudelaire's article was reprinted under his own name in the newspaper *L'Echo* on 23 August 1846, the realization of his own guilt, as well as his awe of Balzac, may have prompted him to add the concluding paragraph: "Should anyone maliciously take this for the scoffing of a small newspaper or for an attack on the glory of the greatest man of our century, he would be shamefully mistaken. I have tried to show that the great poet could find a solution for a bill of exchange as easily as for the most mysterious and complicated novel" (*OC,* 2:1083).

Baudelaire in 1846

Eighteen forty-six was one of Baudelaire's most productive years. In January he published in the *Corsaire-Satan* his second piece of original art criticism, entitled *The Museum of Classics at the Bazar Bonne-Nouvelle.* Among the works of revolutionary art on display were ten paintings by David and eleven by Ingres. Baudelaire wrote enthusiastically about David's *Marat,* which he hailed as "one of the great treasures of modern art"; he gave somewhat qualified praise to Ingres and concluded by regretting the absence of any paintings of Delacroix, hinting that he may have been deliberately omitted out of jealousy.

On 3 March 1846, Baudelaire published in the *Corsaire-Satan* an article entitled "Choix de maximes consolantes," a pastiche of Stendhal's "De l'Amour" that, under its deceptively impersonal humor, tells us much about his relations with Jeanne and perhaps even with Sarah, "la Louchette." Several statements may have been inspired by his former mistress: a thin woman is a "well of mysterious pleasure"; "ugliness has an appeal that stems from thirst for the unknown" and "from the taste for the horrible"—a taste common to both men and women, if only in its incipient form (*OC*, 1:548).

Baudelaire's references to Jeanne, on the other hand, are unmistakable. His complaint to his mother some years later that Jeanne "refused to learn anything" in spite of his offer to be of help is clearly reflected in his advice to young lovers to refrain from teaching spelling to their mistresses: stupidity has its advantages, he claimed. He could only have been thinking of Jeanne's black eyes when he added: "Stupidity is often the ornament of beauty; it gives to those eyes the dull limpidity of blackish pools and the oily calm of tropical seas" (*OC*, 1:549).

That Baudelaire was already aware of Jeanne's infidelity is clear from his admonition offered to those "caught between hereditary and paternal taste for morality and an overpowering desire for a woman deserving scorn." Under a mask of cynical indifference, in the face of the horror inspired by the woman's "base infidelities" and her "shameful secrets accidently discovered," Baudelaire was really stating his own tragic dilemma in the exchange, "virtue and pride cry out; Flee! Nature whispers: Where can you flee?" (*OC*, 1:550). Finally, consistent with the respect that he was always to show his women acquaintances, Baudelaire concludes by cautioning the young lover not to imitate the cheap antics of a Don Juan who makes a fool of himself in the presence of an honorable woman in love with her husband.

On 15 April, a few months after the appearance of the *Maximes,* Baudelaire published in *L'Esprit critique* an essay entitled *Conseils aux jeunes littérateurs* (*Advice to Young Writers*). In it he reveals some of the ideas he was to carry with him throughout life, as well as others he would later renounce, taught by the bitterness of his own experiences. Poetry is "the most honored of all the arts. . . . Every healthy man can do without food for two days, but without poetry—never! . . . Inspiration is . . . the sister of daily work," he adds, although to his genuine dismay, he himself was never able to put his precept into practice. Then, using what seems to be tongue-in-cheek humor to hide his own painful experiences, he advises the aspiring writer: "Never have any creditors; if you insist, pretend to have them." For a mistress, he suggests, in what seems to be an attempt to shock or amuse the reader, choosing "either a prostitute or a stupid woman" (*OC*, 2:19, 20). Ironically enough Jeanne belonged to both categories, as he soon discovered.

To the young man of twenty-five, *guignon* (bad luck) was only an excuse invented by those who fail to succeed; to the Baudelaire of 1852, embittered by poverty and failure, *guignon* will become something as real as it is inexorable. Men like Poe, and presumably like Baudelaire himself, are doomed by fate and bear "the word *guignon* stamped in mysterious letters on their foreheads" (*OC*, 2:249).

The most important of Baudelaire's publications in 1846 was the review, *Le Salon de 1846,* that appeared in May of that year. It proved to be a critical success, revealing a breadth of knowledge ranging from Delacroix to the more obscure American painter George Catlin. With its freshness, enthusiasm, and abundance of ideas, it did much to establish Baudelaire's reputation as an art critic.

La Fanfarlo

1847 began auspiciously with the publication of his novel *La Fanfarlo,* which has proved to be as revealing of its author as the *Maximes* and his correspondence. Both the physical description of Samuel—his eyes shining like drops of coffee, his hair arranged in a Raphaelesque manner—and the psychological motives that explain his conduct and his writing find direct or implicit corroboration in the life and writings of Baudelaire himself. Samuel Cramer was endowed with the same inexplicable lethargy, resulting in a "powerlessness so colossal and so enormous as to be epic"; his nature was "somber streaked with brilliant flashes of light"; he possessed an eclectic taste in reading that, like that of Baudelaire himself, included Swedenborg as well as "more shameful books whose reading is profitable only to minds possessed by an immoderate taste for the truth" (*OC*, 1:552, 553, 555).

No better explanation can be found of Baudelaire's proclivity for appropriating material from others than his description of how his young hero failed to differentiate between what seemed beautiful enough to be his and what was really his: "He was at the same time all the artists that he had studied and all the books that he had read, and yet in spite of this imitative faculty, he remained profoundly original" (*OC*, 1:555). Moreover, Baudelaire's tendency to shock others by his perverse behavior finds an interesting explanation in this somewhat startling confession: "It is hate for everyone and for ourselves that had led us toward these lies. It is from despair at not being noble and handsome by natural means that we have so strangely painted our faces" (*OC*, 1:559).

The parallel between Samuel and Baudelaire is also obvious in their ideas of love. For Samuel, love was "essentially admiration and desire for the beautiful. . . . He loved a human body . . . as if it were a beautiful piece of architecture given movement, and this absolute materialism was not far from the purest idealism" (*OC*, 1:577). This "pure idealism" that Baudelaire seems to confuse with aesthetic pleasure characterizes certain aspects of his love for Jeanne—aspects most apparent in a poem such as "Les Bijoux," in which the poet's pleasure in contemplating his nude mistress is more aesthetic and cerebral than erotic. Far from the lewd verses of some of the lesser poets of his time, "Les Bijoux" has some of the magnificence of the Song of Solomon.

Marie Daubrun

Letters to his mother and to General Aupick indicate that Baudelaire's passionate love for Jeanne had subsided by 1845. In his need for companionship he turned to Marie Daubrun, a young actress best known for her role in *La Belle aux cheveux d'or* (1847). Just when Baudelaire made the acquaintance of the lovely green-eyed actress remains something of an enigma. What is certain is that she played an important role in his life from 1850 to 1860; she may even have become his mistress somewhere between 1855 and 1859. In the meantime, Baudelaire did everything possible to help Marie advance in her career, even soliciting the aid of George Sand, whose works and ideas he despised.

The poet Banville replaced Baudelaire in Marie's affections in 1852. When she decided to accompany the seriously ill poet to Nice, Baudelaire, angry and hurt, composed the poem "A une Madone," in which the mingling of religious and erotic elements is resolved in a violent and sadistic conclusion. Its tone clashes strangely with the note of tenderness and affection that characterizes most of the poems inspired by the actress. The rift between Banville and Baudelaire, however, was not of long duration; their warm friendship was resumed and continued until Baudelaire's death in 1867.

A Strange Interlude

In 1848 and 1849 Baudelaire played a minor but decided role in the Revolution of 1848. This period of political activism, prompted both by his affinity for the causes of social justice and his growing dislike for his stepfather, formed a strange interlude in the life of the otherwise apolitical poet. Some years later, in a few provocative notes in his *Journaux intimes,* the poet himself reveals his state of mind during that period: "My intoxication in 1848. What was the nature of that intoxication? Taste for vengeance, *natu-*

ral pleasure in destruction. Literary intoxication, recollection of things read"
(*OC,* 1:679).

The taste for vengeance was undeniably motivated by his growing dislike
for his stepfather, who personified the society he felt had rejected him. This
was further exacerbated by Aupick's growing importance—he had been
promoted to general—and his own failure to achieve success. All his
pent-up anger erupted during the uprising of 24 February, when Baudelaire
was seen by his friend Jules Buisson marching through the streets, brandishing a new rifle, and shouting: "We must go and shoot General Aupick!"[6]

In his "natural pleasure in destruction," Baudelaire was obviously referring to his firm belief in original sin and to his conviction that man derives a
certain pleasure from the conscious awareness of his wrongdoing. A more
valid and satisfactory explanation of the poet's state of mind may be found
in his comment, "Literary intoxication, recollections of things read." In
1847, Baudelaire had become intensely interested in the question of social
injustice, which was being hotly debated in France at that time. He spent
much time in reading Robert de Lamennais, Pierre Leroux, Charles Fourier,
Louis Blanc, and especially Joseph-Pierre Proudhon, who, among others,
were calling attention to the social evils of the day and suggesting various
types of reform. Though less involved in the social struggle than many of his
contemporaries, Baudelaire was far from indifferent to the movement.

In 1848 the poet supported the revolutionary cause in several ways: he
took his place at the barricades on 24 February, became a member of the
Société Républicaine Centrale, and, with his friends Champfleury and
Toubin, founded the socialist newspaper *Le Salut public* that, for want of
funds, was to publish only two issues (27 February and 1 or 2 March).
Moreover, in the electoral meetings held in April, he directed questions to
Alphonse Esquiros and Arsène Houssaye that indicate he had more knowledge of certain issues pertaining to political economy than either of the two
candidates. The fact that Baudelaire served (10 April to 6 May) on the edi-
torial staff of *La Tribune nationale,* a moderate Republican newspaper, is
not necessarily an indication of vacillation on his part. As Marcel Ruff has
pointed out, *La Tribune* was voicing opinions as advanced as those of *Le
Salut public* and was becoming more and more forceful in its opposition to
the government.[7] Its final number, in fact, not only gave cautious backing
to Proudhon's proposal for a bank of exchange that was to institute free
credit, but also contained a long quotation from the newspaper that
Proudhon published himself.

A few months later, on 20 October, Baudelaire became the editor-in-
chief of the *Représentant de l'Indre* in Châteauroux. His stay was brief. His

deliberately provocative actions and words so scandalized the collaborators of the newspaper that they soon parted company, and Baudelaire returned to Paris.

Baudelaire and Proudhon

Although Baudelaire had been intrigued by the ideas of Fourier, it was Joseph-Pierre Proudhon who most influenced his thinking. Given their differences in taste and personalities, Baudelaire's friendship and admiration for Proudhon is somewhat incongruous; however, we know that he must have read Proudhon's ponderous *Philosophie de la misère* (*Philosophy of Poverty*) with approval. He copied a long passage on the problem of aesthetics and morality into his notebook, and modeled the questions he asked in the electoral meetings of 1848 on ones that Proudhon had discussed in that same treatise.

In 1848 Baudelaire initiated closer contact with Proudhon when he wrote two letters warning him of possible attempts against his life and urging him to take steps to protect himself. The first, dated 21 August, is marked by an almost naive enthusiasm that is quite uncharacteristic of the poet. The second, written the same or the following day, is even more insistent in its warning: "You may be *assassinated*. It is a real plot" (*Corr.,* 1:151).

It was evidently soon afterward that Baudelaire encountered Proudhon in the office of the newspaper *Le Représentant du peuple* and accompanied him to a small restaurant where, according to the poet's account, Proudhon talked enthusiastically, "introducing me . . . to his plans and projects" (*Corr.,* 2:470). They also met occasionally at the *Brasserie Andler* where, for a few years, the artist Gustave Courbet and his friends used to gather each evening. Courbet—who, incidentally, had done a vignette for the second and final edition of *Le Salut public*—had also become an intimate friend of Champfleury and Proudhon.

In 1849 Baudelaire's enthusiasm for Proudhon's ideas had not lessened, as Delacroix reveals in his account of a visit from the poet in his *Journal*.[8] This enthusiasm was also reflected in two essays published in 1851. "Proudhon is a writer whom Europe will always envy us," Baudelaire wrote in *Les Drames et les romans honnêtes*"; in his essay on Pierre Dupont he not only repudiated, for the first and only time, his admiration for René and Obermann, he also adopted the philosophy of action that was being preached by the socialist reformer. That he was actually thinking of

Proudhon is proved by the four lines immediately following that he quotes from "ce sublime mouvement de Proudhon" (*OC,* 2:34).

This intellectual affinity, however, did not carry over to the personal level. Years later, writing to congratulate Sainte-Beuve who, after Proudhon's death in 1865, had published a series of four laudatory articles based on the reformer's life and correspondence, Baudelaire added: "I read him a lot, and knew him a little. Pen in hand, he wasn't a *bad sort;* but he wasn't and never had been, even on paper, a *Dandy!* That's what I shall never pardon in him" (*Corr.,* 2:563). Baudelaire's reservations were obviously based on Proudhon's crude manners and on the fact that the reformer, as Gerstle Mack has observed, could never see anything in a picture except a sociological tract.[9]

Baudelaire and Poe

In 1852 Baudelaire's admiration for the works of Edgar Allan Poe was transformed into a veritable passion. He had actually discovered the American writer as early as 1847, after reading a translation of *The Black Cat* by Isabelle Meunier, English-born wife of the socialist leader Victor Meunier. In fact, Baudelaire himself had published a translation of *Mesmeric Revelation* in July 1848.

It was not until 1852 that Baudelaire published his first essay on Poe himself in the March and April issues of the *Revue de Paris.* After a long delay, during which his knowledge of English improved, in 1856 he published his first volume of Poe translations, under the title of *Histoires extraordinaires;* its preface was a long essay based on his articles of 1852. A year later, in 1857, he published a second volume of translations, entitled *Nouvelles Histoires extraordinaires,* prefaced by another essay that has proven to be one of his most important critical studies. In it he set forth at length for the first time the principles that formed the core of his own aesthetic doctrine.

His interest in Poe never ceased. He continued translating the works of Poe until 1865, two years before his death, when the fifth and final volume of his translations was finally published. Baudelaire's three essays and even more his translations of Poe were responsible for the American writer's enormous popularity in France and other countries of the non-English-speaking world.

It was not until 1952 that Professor W. T. Bandy made the startling discovery that the 1852 essay on Poe was largely a plagiarism of two obituary articles that had been published in the *Southern Literary Messenger.*[10] From an American correspondent, William Wilberforce Mann, who had come to Paris during the 1850s, Baudelaire had obtained copies of the *Messenger* in which two obituary notices on Poe appeared. From one of them, an article by John M. Daniel that was published in March 1850, Baudelaire translated almost word for word twenty-five pages of the forty-page essay. Baudelaire had also borrowed considerably—although far less extensively than from Daniel—from a Poe obituary by John R. Thompson, printed in the November 1849 *Messenger.*

Bandy explains that in 1852 Baudelaire had only the Wiley and Putnam edition (1845) of Poe and that he had seen neither the Redfield edition nor the Grisvold *Memoir* at the time he wrote the essay. Moreover, Baudelaire had complained in letters to his mother that Jeanne was making life impossible for him and that, as a consequence, he was forced to work all night or go to a restaurant or café in order to concentrate.

Whatever the reason for the plagiary, Professor Bandy's discovery has helped to solve the question of the extent of Poe's influence on *Les Fleurs du mal.* As he points out, "It would appear that virtually all the poems which were published in the first edition of 1857 were written before 1850. If, as late as 1853, Baudelaire had read . . . only three or four of Poe's poems and none of his critical articles, it stands to reason that such critics as Lemonnier and Rhodes, who have minimized the possibility of such influence, are on very solid ground."[11]

The Blonde Venus

In 1852 Baudelaire decided to break with Jeanne, with whom life was becoming more and more intolerable. In a letter to his mother he describes the situation in words that recall the prediction made by Samuel Cramer five years earlier: ". . . passions are deceiving, and there must come a day when the idol, to more clear-sighted eyes, is an object, not of hate, but of surprise and scorn" (*OC,* 1:561).

Desperately in need of money, moving from one cheap hotel to another in order to escape his creditors, depressed and lonely after his separation from Jeanne and tortured by his lack of success, Baudelaire turned to the charming and warmhearted Mme de Sabatier for the sympathy and understanding he so badly needed. Gautier brought him to one of the Sunday dinners she gave in her apartment on the rue Frochet, where she had been established by her lover Count Alfred Mosselman, a wealthy Jewish banker. Here Baudelaire could mingle with members of the literary and art world, including Flaubert, Maxime DuCamp, the sculptor Auguste Clésinger,

Ernest Feydeau, and of course Gautier himself. Here he was able to momentarily forget the miserable existence he was leading and enjoy the only "luxe, calme et volupté" that he was ever to know.

In gratitude for her thoughtfulness and kindness, Baudelaire sent Mme Sabatier a number of anonymous letters and poems; "la présidente," as she was affectionately called, knew very well they could only have come from him. Unfortunately, Mme Sabatier failed to note that both his poems and letters were almost completely lacking in sensuality and were filled only with the author's gratitude and admiration. In fact, from the very beginning of their friendship, Baudelaire had made every effort in both his poetry and his letters to prove to Mme Sabatier that his devotion was entirely platonic. His insistence on anonymity may have been another pretext for keeping their relationship on formal terms. A letter he sent her on 8 May 1854 seems calculated to set up certain barriers between them and to discourage Mme Sabatier from thinking of him as a suitor. He subtly reminds her of her "duties" elsewhere, warmly praises her lover, Count Mosselman, speaks of the respect in which she was held by all, and frankly admits that he himself is an "egoist" who finds in her a rich source of inspiration. This last letter was accompanied by one of his loveliest and most idealistic poems, known today as "Hymne," which was followed by the simple but telling statement: "Forgive me, I ask no more of you."

Between February 1854 and August 1857, Baudelaire seems to have had little or no contact with Mme Sabatier. In fact, in December 1854, Baudelaire wrote his mother telling her that he intended to return "dans le concubinage" either with Jeanne or "chez l'autre" (Marie Daubrun). In the meantime, he was continuing his work on Poe, including a prose translation of "The Raven" (29 July 1854). On 1 June 1855, he experienced a moment of triumph when the distinguished journal the *Revue des deux mondes* published eighteen of the poems that were later to appear in *Les Fleurs du mal*. Unfortunately, little attention was paid them until five months later, when Louis Goudall published a scathing review in the 5 November *Figaro*.

New Disappointments

In 1855, an art exhibition that was held as part of the *Exposition universelle* being held in Paris aroused Baudelaire's interest. The jury had refused the paintings submitted by his old friend Gustave Courbet, including the magnificent *L'Atelier* (The Studio), in which the poet and a few other friends are portrayed. With his usual stubborn determination, Courbet set up his own one-man show in what he called the Pavilion of Realism facing the juried Salon.

Despite his fondness for Courbet, Baudelaire had come to reject Realism, and was disturbed and angry that his inclusion in the painting would associate him with a movement that he so heartily detested. In his two articles on the exhibit, the first (3 June) was devoted to Delacroix, and the second (12 August) to Ingres. He made one passing reference to Courbet in the second.

Baudelaire had planned and had even begun an article "Puisque Réalisme il y a" ("Since It Is a Question of Realism") in which he intended to explain his antipathy to Realism and to answer Champfleury's letter-manifesto defending Courbet. The essay was never finished, perhaps in part because the author hesitated to hurt two of his best and oldest friends. From that time on, the poet saw less and less of Courbet, although they remained on friendly terms. Baudelaire's influence on Courbet may be seen in a number of his paintings, especially in *Le Sommeil* (known in English-speaking countries as *Women Asleep*), inspired by the poem "Les Femmes damnées." In 1862, the poet-critic praised the artist for "contributing not a little to re-establishing a taste for simplicity and for his disinterested, absolute love of painting" (*OC*, 2:737).

The year 1856 was in Baudelaire's own words "the most cruel of all." Sainte-Beuve, whom the poet sincerely admired and praised, reneged on a promise to review his translation of Poe's *Histoires Extraordinaires,* thus depriving Baudelaire of support that could have proved invaluable. In the meanwhile, Baudelaire's ever-increasing debts, his endless trips to Neuilly to beg M. Ancelle for money, and his misunderstandings with his mother all increased his gloom and irascibility and led him to quarrel more bitterly with Jeanne, with whom he had had a rapprochement in 1854. This time it was Jeanne who decided to leave; almost beside himself with grief and rage, the poet turned once more to his mother for help, despite their strained relationship. He confessed all his unhappiness in a letter of 11 September 1856, accusing himself of insensitivity in language echoed in the poem "L'Héautontimoromenos"—which may well have been written at that time—and expressing his horror at the thought of the lonely years ahead "without a family, without friends, without a mistress, endless years of loneliness and troubles—and nothing to fill my heart" (*OC*, 1:357).

Les Fleurs du mal

On 25 June 1857, Baudelaire's volume of poetry *Les Fleurs du mal,* published by his close friend Poulet-Malassis, went on sale. After leading a somewhat Bohemian life in Paris, Poulet-Malassis had returned to Alençon after the death of his father to take over his press, one of the best in the country. More a man of letters than a businessman, Poulet-Malassis went on to reform the art of typography in France and had already begun publishing books that today are sought by bibliophiles everywhere.

The publication was to have disastrous results. On 15 July, a devastating review by Gustave Bourdin appeared in the *Figaro,* which described the book as "a hospital open to all the aberrations of the human mind and to all the putrescence of the human heart."[12] On 12 July, a second denunciatory article in the *Figaro* led to the prosecution of both Baudelaire and Poulet-Malassis for offending public morality. In a desperate attempt to avoid prosecution Baudelaire begged Sainte-Beuve for a favorable review, but once again the critic failed to come to his rescue, even though he was known to have praised *Les Fleurs du mal* in private. His colleague Thierry did write a highly complimentary review, even comparing Baudelaire to Dante, but to no avail. Brought to court, Baudelaire was condemned for having offended public morality through the sordid realism of his poetry. The poet was fined three hundred francs; Poulet-Malassis, two hundred. In addition, six of the poems were banned from the volume. As the result of an appeal to the Empress Eugénie, Baudelaire's fine was reduced to fifty francs.

In a last-minute attempt to avoid prosecution, Baudelaire wrote to Mme Sabatier after a silence of several years. Although he tried to explain his silence by renewing his praise for her charm and beauty, it is clear that his real intention was the hope that she might be able to sway the decision of the judges. The very fact that he admitted he needed her help and that he gave her the judges' names is proof that he believed she might have some influence.

Touched by his letter, Mme Sabatier misinterpreted the nature of his feelings and, deciding to take the initiative, wrote to arrange a meeting. What took place remains unclear but, judging from the letters exchanged afterward, Baudelaire evidently failed to respond to her offer of a liaison, whether from an unresolved Oedipus complex, from a lack of passionate love on his part, or perhaps even from fear of his own inadequacies.

Mme Sabatier herself seems to have divined the real reason, and she was undoubtedly right. In a letter to the poet she wrote: "Do you want me to tell you what I really think? It is that you do not love me. . . ."[13] From that time on, Baudelaire did his best to put their friendship on a more formal basis and for a time ceased to attend her Sunday dinners. His letters became more impersonal, though still filled with gracious compliments.

A New Beginning

Baudelaire's discouragement grew more marked as the year drew to a close. After Gen. Aupick's death in April 1857, his mother left Paris to live in their charming small house in Honfleur, the Maison-Joujou. Genuinely moved and perhaps even somewhat conscience-stricken by her son's heart-breaking letters, she finally invited him to join her in Honfleur. She had read *Les Fleurs du mal* and to her astonishment found, as she wrote to her stepson Claude, that the book contained "some marvelous verses of great purity of language and simplicity of form," despite "some horrible and offensive descriptions."[14]

It was not until January 1859 that Baudelaire was finally able to leave for Honfleur. In addition to other nagging problems, his desire to pay his debts before leaving Paris and Ancelle's insistence on making a careful investigation before advancing any money forced the poet to keep postponing the trip. In the meantime his close friend Babou—who had suggested *Les Fleurs du mal* as a title for his volume of poetry—published an article in *La Revue française* that attacked Sainte-Beuve for praising Feydeau's mediocre novel *Fanny* while failing to recognize the merit of Baudelaire's poetry. Baudelaire was deeply disturbed not only because he feared Sainte-Beuve would think the article had been inspired by him, but also because he was genuinely fond of the critic, despite the latter's failure ever to come to his assistance.

Baudelaire's joy over living at Honfleur was short-lived. In April 1859 he learned that Jeanne had suffered a paralytic stroke and had been taken to a hospital in Paris. Although passionate love on his part had long since died away, he was to continue to feel responsible for her welfare all his life and to do his utmost to help her financially. Jeanne, on the other hand, felt no qualms in taking advantage of his kindness; on this occasion she extorted money from him by pretending she had not received the sum he had sent for paying her hospital expenses.

While staying in Honfleur, in the house overlooking the estuary, Baudelaire was to experience his last and most important creative period. There he composed some of the best poems of the second edition of *Les Fleurs du mal,* among them "Le Voyage," the longest and greatest of his compositions. During his stay at Honfleur Baudelaire also wrote his brilliant *Salon de 1859.* During a sojourn in Paris from the beginning of March until late April, he had made a quick visit to the exhibition. On his return to Honfleur, he wrote Nadar that he had composed the *Salon* without even having seen it. Two days later, in a second letter, he admitted that he had indeed seen the exhibit, but on one occasion *only*, and that he had spent his time looking for what was new to him, relying only on a quick glance and on the brochure for discussing the artists with whose works he was already acquainted.

Baudelaire and Méryon

At the Salon of 1859, Baudelaire discovered some somber and mysterious etchings of Paris done by an obscure, poverty-stricken artist named Charles Méryon. Intrigued by the beauty of Méryon's work, Baudelaire sought out the artist and did his utmost to help him find a publisher for his etchings. Méryon, who was subject to intermittent attacks of insanity and had recently returned from a stay in the asylum at Charenton, was unable to appreciate the time and energy Baudelaire spent in helping him sell his works. When his condition worsened, Méryon was obliged to return to Charenton; he died there in 1868, a year after the death of his benefactor. That his works live on is largely due to Baudelaire's efforts to bring them to the attention of the public.

Baudelaire and Manet

Baudelaire's unselfish interest in all those who, like Méryon, had genuine talent was one of his finest characteristics. It was true of his friendship for Manet, who became one of his closest friends and was known to be one of the artist's constant companions, especially in the late 1850s and early 1860s. Early in the 1860s, Baudelaire would often accompany Manet in his daily visits to the Tuileries gardens, where the artist liked to make studies in the open air. Evidently poet and artist occasionally vied with each other in treating similar subjects, as in the case of Baudelaire's prose poem "Les Veuves" ("Widows"), reminiscent of Manet's portrayal of a similar crowd in *La Musique aux Tuileries*.

Poet and artist were to remain close friends through life. Before leaving for Brussels, it was to Manet that Baudelaire turned for advice and aid; during his stay in Brussels, the artist continued to be of great assistance. He not only acted as Baudelaire's intermediary from time to time but also lent him five hundred francs, despite the fact that the poet had been unable to repay the thousand francs he had lent him two years earlier.

After Baudelaire's return to Paris and during his stay in the nursing home, their friendship continued. Manet was one of a group of friends who used to take the ailing poet to lunch with them in the early days of his illness. Weak and speechless, Baudelaire could only listen and occasionally interrupt their conversation with the only word he could pronounce: *"Crénom! Crénom!"* ("Damn it! Damn it!"). On one occasion when Manet was unable to accompany them, Baudelaire, deeply disappointed, called out from the garden where he was waiting: "Manet! Manet!" "That took the place of the usual damn it," Nadar wrote to the artist.[15]

Baudelaire has often been blamed for failing to devote an entire essay to Manet when the artist was so badly in need of support. The poet-critic's failure to do so may well have been the result of his deteriorating health or even more of his inability, as he wrote his mother, to find a journal that would publish his work. Moreover, before leaving for Brussels, Baudelaire had seen only a few of Manet's paintings. He obviously had certain reservations about them that would have presented a number of difficulties, obliging him to either ignore or contradict some of the aesthetic beliefs that he had previously expressed. Whatever the case, Baudelaire did his utmost to encourage Manet and to influence all those who could be of any help in his behalf. Moreover, he did come to the artist's defense in two critical articles, *L'eau-forte est à la mode (Etching Is in Fashion)* and *Peintres et aquafortistes (Painters and Etchers)*, both published in 1862.

Baudelaire and Constantin Guys

It was also in 1859 that Baudelaire made the acquaintance of an eccentric artist, Constantin Guys (1805–92) who, like the poet, was fascinated by life in a great city and found his inspiration in its crowded streets and various haunts. A former art correspondent for the *London Illustrated News,* for which he had made sketches during visits to Spain, Turkey, and the Crimea, he spent his last years in Paris, where he did delightful sketches based on every aspect of Parisian life.

A close friend of the famous photographer Nadar (to whom Guys bequeathed his portfolio), admired by Delacroix for his watercolors, praised by Gautier (who owned about sixty of his sketches), Guys found in Baudelaire a kindred soul whose taste for modernity equaled his own. Guys was the subject of Baudelaire's essay *Le Peintre de la vie moderne (The Painter of Modern Life)*, which, although written between 1859 and 1860, was first published in 1863. Forbidden by the overly modest Guys to use his name, Baudelaire was forced to refer to him only by his initials throughout the essay.

The fact that Baudelaire devoted this long and remarkable essay to Guys rather than Daumier or Manet has often been cited as a mistake in judgment. It is important to note, however, that in the opening paragraphs the poet-critic indirectly yet deliberately categorizes Guys as one of those "poetae minores" whose work contains "du bon, du solide, and du délicieux"—hardly expressions of extravagant praise.[16] Whereas he likens Guys to Gavarni and Deveria, he elsewhere characterizes Delacroix as an "unrivaled artist" comparable to Raphael and Veronese.

Baudelaire's failure to use Manet as the subject of his essay is explained by the fact that Manet's production in 1859 and 1860 was scanty and lacked the authentic modern expression to justify his being hailed as the painter of modern life. Daumier, on the other hand, was highly regarded by Baudelaire—almost as highly as Delacroix. In fact, Baudelaire was among the very first to publicly recognize that Daumier not only ranked among the very greatest of his time, but that he actually drew as well as Ingres and better than Delacroix (*OC*, 2:356). By choosing Guys as opposed to Daumier, however, Baudelaire was able to include chapters on dandyism, on makeup, and on women—subjects he had originally intended for a general study on the painting of manners.

Baudelaire and Wagner

The *Salon de 1859* and his essays on Constantin Guys and Richard Wagner represent the final steps in the evolution of Baudelaire's artistic thought. They are of special interest not only for their expression of his general aesthetic ideas but also because they are superb examples of how he applied those ideas.

The essay on Wagner was Baudelaire's only excursion into the field of music. Although he had made no formal study of music he was sensitive to its beauty and power, as is clearly evident in *Les Fleurs du mal*. Influenced no doubt by Gérard De Nerval and Champfleury, the poet had become interested in Wagner's music as early as 1849. It was only in 1860, however, that his enthusiasm was transformed into passionate admiration comparable to that which he had felt for Poe and Delacroix.

In 1859, Wagner came to Paris to direct three concerts that would be performed at the Salle Ventadour in 1860. For the most part critics were hostile, whereas public opinion was more favorable. Sensing the greatness of the music, Baudelaire wrote the composer an enthusiastic letter that may almost be considered a first draft of the article that he was to write a year later after he attended a performance of the opera *Tannhäuser*. Wagner sought Baudelaire out—the poet-critic had given no address—and invited him to attend the soirées held every Wednesday evening for his many friends.

The essay on Wagner, dated 18 March 1861, appeared on 1 April in the *Revue Européenne*, about two weeks after the opening night of the opera *Tannhäuser*, on 13 March. The major part of the article had evidently been written before Baudelaire had actually seen the performance. The last pages were added after the first performance, when the opera had already been declared a failure. The essay with its postscript, dated 8 April, was published as a brochure on 4 May 1861. It is one of Baudelaire's most remarkable essays, appealing mainly to "poetic readers." To supply the technical information that he lacked, he included extensive quotations from Liszt, Berlioz, and Wagner himself, whose articles he had already read.

Not only did Baudelaire recognize in Wagner the grandeur that he sought in art, he also discovered that the theme of *Tannhäuser* was identical to his own belief in the duality of man: "the struggle of the two principles that have chosen the human heart as their chief battleground—flesh against spirit, hell against heaven, Satan against God" (*OC*, 2:794). Moreover, he found in Wagner an artist capable of creating through music alone, unaided by words, the suggestive magic that he had defined about 1859 or 1860 as "a suggestive magic containing at one and the same time the object and the subject, the world exterior to the artist and the artist himself" (*OC*, 2:598).

Baudelaire and Liszt

Through Wagner and his wife Baudelaire first met the brilliant composer and pianist Franz Liszt, who was to inspire some of his finest poems. Baudelaire and Liszt became close friends, and in his prose poem "Le Thyrse," dedicated to Liszt, Baudelaire reveals a warmth of personal feeling that is seldom found in his work—not even in his hommage paid to Poe, Delacroix, and Wagner. Writer and composer were both intensely interested in gypsy life and found inspiration in their picturesque way of living— Baudelaire in "Les Bohémiens en voyage" and his prose poem "Les Vocations," Liszt in the wildly passionate gypsy melodies of his native Hungary. Even in Brussels Baudelaire did not forget his charismatic friend, as we know from a letter he sent Manet asking him to send the "rapsodie de Lizt" [*sic*].

Les Paradis artificiels

In May of 1860, Poulet-Malassis published Baudelaire's *Paradis artificiels,* composed of two articles that first appeared consecutively in the *Revue contemporaine.* The first, entitled *Haschisch,* had been published as early as September 1858; the second, known as *Opium,* had not been completed until January 1860, much to the exasperation of the editor. Based not on his own experiences but on de Quincy's *Confessions of an Opium Eater, Les Paradis* proved very difficult to write. Baudelaire solved the problem by extensively quoting passages from the original and summarizing the rest in his own words.

Though the book received a few favorable reviews, on the whole it was either ignored or sharply criticized. As usual, Sainte-Beuve made no effort to come to the author's rescue. Baudelaire's intention in writing *Les Paradis* had been to condemn rather than to commend the use of drugs. In his own early, carefree years he had experimented with drugs primarily as a means of procuring sensuous pleasure and enlarging his experience. As he grew older, especially during his stay in Brussels, he came to rely on them either as a means of escape or of relieving the intense, often excruciating pain related to his illness. By the time he was writing *Les Paradis* he had already come to consider the practice dangerous and demoralizing. In fact, in the opening pages of *Haschisch* he had even cited, as one aspect of his study, the "implied immorality in this pursuit of a false ideal" (*OC,* 1:403).

Most critics approved Baudelaire's moral stand on the subject. Flaubert, found much to praise in the book, but was not in agreement with some of its ideas: "It seems to me . . . you have insisted (and several times at that) too much (?) on the *Evil Spirit.* One senses, as it were, a kind of Catholic leavening here and there."[17]

Baudelaire's reply to Flaubert is of the greatest importance, for it explains much of what he wrote in both his poetry and prose: "I was struck by your observation and, after plumbing very carefully the depths of my past reveries, I realized that I have always been obsessed by the impossibility of accounting for some of man's sudden acts and thoughts except by the hypothesis of the intervention of an evil force outside himself. That is a tremendous admission for which I won't blush, even with the whole nineteenth century standing against me" (*Corr.,* 2:53).

It is not the only time that Baudelaire affirmed his belief in some evil force outside of man. In his *Journaux intimes* he noted: "There are in every man, and at all times, two simultaneous impulses, the one toward God, the other toward Satan" (*OC,* 1:682). And in his introductory poem to *Les Fleurs du mal,* he affirms unequivocally: "It is the Devil who holds the strings that move us!"

A Candidate for the French Academy

Early in February 1861 the second edition of *Les Fleurs du mal* was published. It contained one hundred poems from the 1857 edition and excluded the six that had been condemned by the court. Of the 126 poems in the new volume, 31 were new pieces published after 1857.

Meanwhile, it was becoming quite apparent to Baudelaire that his hopes of obtaining financial security and paying his debts were becoming increasingly untenable. The fact that Poulet-Malassis was on the verge of bankruptcy made his situation more precarious and set him to dreaming of some miracle that could save him. A panacea for his ills, he believed, would be membership in the French Academy. It would not only help sell his books, it would also justify him in the eyes of his mother and of the reading public.

In December 1861 Baudelaire wrote to the secretary of the French Academy declaring his candidacy. The announcement caused a great stir in the literary world and led many to believe that he was merely trying to create a scandal. Of all the members of the Academy to whom Baudelaire paid the customary visits required of all candidates, it was the author Alfred de Vigny, ill and dying of cancer, who alone seemed to realize Baudelaire's genius. Despite his sincere admiration for the rare beauty of the poetry, he advised its author to withdraw his candidacy, realizing that it would only result in disappointment and humiliation.

This time Sainte-Beuve, in his official capacity, was obliged to comment in *Le Constitutionnel* on the candidates for election. Whether through prudence or through a genuine lack of sympathetic understanding, he characterized Baudelaire's position in literature with circumspection and damning praise. Baudelaire, he maintained, had built for himself "a strange Kiosk . . . at the extreme point of the Kamchatka of Romanticism" . . . which "I call Baudelaire's country Pleasure-House" (*Corr.,* 2:767).

The poet seemed unaware of the dubious nature of his commendation and was overjoyed that Sainte-Beuve had described him as "a polite, respectful, exemplary candidate, a nice young man, refined in his speech, a perfect gentleman in every respect." As he wrote Sainte-Beuve, he had been deeply hurt over the years by the fact that he was generally believed to be "surly and impossible" and a drunkard "who smelled badly," as one woman had told him in surprise on meeting the polite and impeccably neat poet for the first time (*Corr.,* 2:219).

On the advice of Sainte-Beuve and de Vigny, Baudelaire withdrew his candidacy, convinced that further struggle was useless. His deep disappointment was to be followed by one disaster after another. Poulet-Malassis, whom he had counted on to publish his works, was arrested and imprisoned for debt; although Baudelaire owed him 500 francs, he was unable to come to his rescue. In the meantime, he had discovered that the "brother" who had been living with Jeanne at his expense was really her lover and that in the hope of obtaining more money she had written Mme Aupick, complaining that she had been abandoned and left to starve.

In the meantime, the poet's health was rapidly deteriorating. In his *Journaux intimes* a pathetic notation reveals his state of mind and serves as a foreboding of what was to come: "Today the 23rd of January, 1862, I experienced a strange warning: I felt passing over me *the wind of the wing of madness*" (*OC*, 1:668). Letters to his mother confirm the gravity of his condition: nightmares, anxieties, prolonged lethargies, fear of dying or of seeing his mother die, fear of going to sleep, and a horror of waking up. Sitting in his cold dark room on the last day of December 1863, he wrote Mme Aupick of his intention to go to Brussels, ostensibly to give a series of lectures but in reality to seek a publisher for his collected works. He had also been obliged to sign a disastrous contract with Michel Lévy in which he rashly sold all future rights to his Poe translations, including those on which he was still working. To add to the irony, Baudelaire was to receive nothing from the sale, for Lévy had agreed to divide the proceeds among the poet's creditors as soon as he received the fifth volume.

Brussels

On 24 April 1863, Baudelaire left Paris for Brussels. His visit there was to result in further disasters. His lecture series, except for the first on Delacroix, proved to be a fiasco. He was unable to find a publisher for his works, and his intention to write a book on Belgium was never fully carried out. After his death, it was found to be only a collection of bitterly savage notes, filled with hatred and vituperation. In Brussels, the poet's health worsened—he suffered from frightful headaches, cold sweats, prolonged stupor, and dizziness that at times prevented him from walking or even standing. Unable at times to leave his room, Baudelaire waited in vain for news from his literary agent Julien Lemer, whose duty it was to persuade the Garnier brothers to publish the poet-critic's complete works.

With no word from Lemer, both Manet and Ancelle undertook to act as Baudelaire's intermediaries. Manet's warm letters gave further proof of his sincere friendship; Baudelaire in turn sought to encourage the artist, who was disheartened by the unfavorable response of critics and public alike to his painting *Olympia*.

Baudelaire's former antagonism toward Ancelle was transformed at this stage of his life into real affection. Even when Ancelle made mistakes, the poet begged his mother to promise to say nothing: "That poor man has enough troubles finding his way around in business matters that are new to him" (*Corr.*, 2:594). In the meantime Ancelle, who according to Baudelaire knew "as much about literature as elephants know about dancing a bolero," had gone to a lecture by the poet Paul Eugène Louis Deschanels and wrote his ward about the murmurs of admiration that arose in the audience when the lecturer read certain poems of Baudelaire. Baudelaire was secretly pleased, though he chided his guardian for listening to such a "numskull" (*Corr.*, 2:610).

Of even greater importance must have been the news that Sainte-Beuve had written him about a month earlier. The critic told him of a series of enthusiastic articles published in *L'Art* (16 November and 20 and 23 December 1865) written by an obscure young poet, Paul Verlaine. Sainte-Beuve added: "If you were here, you would become, whether you wished it or not, an authority, an oracle, a consulting poet."[18]

In the meantime, Baudelaire had become a frequent visitor at the home of Victor Hugo, who had gone into exile to avoid repercussions from Louis Napoleon whom he had attacked in both *Napoléon le petit* and *Les Châtiments*. After his first visit in May 1865 and for some time afterward, he felt only dislike for the entire family. "Victor Hugo," he wrote his mother, "tired and bored me a great deal . . . Mme Hugo is half idiotic, and her three sons are complete fools" (*Corr.*, 2:495). Baudelaire was soon to rescind his judgment of Mme Hugo and actually became very fond of the frail old woman. Not long before his stroke (16 February), he wrote his mother that "Mme Hugo, who seemed only ridiculous to me at first, is decidedly a good woman" (*Corr.*, 2:599). He became a frequent guest at their home and when at times he was too ill to leave his room, Madame Hugo sent him friendly notes assuring him that a place was always set for him at their table. When Baudelaire was left helpless after his stroke of apoplexy, both Victor Hugo and his wife sought the best medical advice available.

A New Crisis

In July 1865 news came from Poulet-Malassis that sent Baudelaire rushing to Paris in hope of borrowing money. In desperate financial straits, Poulet-Malassis was about to sell the mortgage of five thousand francs which the poet had given him in 1862 in lieu of paying a debt of two hundred francs. Had Poulet sold the mortgage, Baudelaire would have lost the rights to three volumes of his most salable books and been faced with complete ruin.

Arriving in Paris late at night, tired, distraught, without baggage, he encountered Catulle Mendès coming out of the Gard du Nord. Suspecting that the poet was without money, Mendès invited him to spend the night at his apartment. That night Mendès awoke in the dark and heard Baudelaire weeping in the next room. The following morning he was gone, leaving only a note of farewell.

In Honfleur, Mme Aupick drew from her son the story of his sad plight and, realizing the seriousness of the problem, insisted on borrowing money to pay the debt. Released from his torturing fears, Baudelaire returned to Brussels, where his medical symptoms soon grew more alarming.

Receiving no word from Lemer, the poet decided to return to Paris once more, hoping to draw up a contract with the Garnier brothers. Before leaving, he accompanied Poulet-Malassis and their good friend the Belgian artist Félicien Rops to Namur to revisit the lovely Jesuit church of Saint-Loup; with what seems like prescient knowledge, Baudelaire had once described it as "the interior of a catafalque embroidered in *black* in *rose* and in *silver*" (*OC,* 2:951–2). Suddenly, while examining the carving, Baudelaire stumbled and fell. To his friends he maintained he had slipped, but Poulet-Malassis, observing his strangely quiet and sad manner, realized the matter was more serious.

Back in Brussels, Baudelaire continued to have attacks from which he was never to recover. One night, after dining with the photographer Neyt, he abruptly left the restaurant. The worried Neyt found him later sitting in the Taverne Royale, haggard and dazed, a glass of brandy before him. After helping the poet home, Neyt returned the next morning and found him lying on his bed fully dressed, unable to speak, with the lamp still burning. The doctor who was summoned gave a diagnosis of aphasia resulting from a stroke.

When Baudelaire's condition worsened, Ancelle hastened to Brussels and had the poet placed in a Catholic nursing home where he scandalized the sisters in charge by repeating in impotent rage "*Crénom*" ("Damn it")—the only word he could pronounce. After a stay of two and a half months, first in the nursing home and then in his hotel, Baudelaire returned to Paris, where he entered the clinic of Emil Duval.

Visited often by his friends and listening to Mme Manet and his old friend Mme Meurice play Wagner's music for him, Baudelaire at first seemed happy and content. However, as time dragged on with no signs of improvement, he became more and more depressed and seemed to lose the will to live. On 31 August 1867, about eleven o'clock in the morning, he died peacefully in his mother's arms. He was 46 years old.

In death as in life, Baudelaire was pursued by the ill luck that had always seemed to dog his footsteps. Only a hundred persons attended the funeral; of these, about sixty followed the procession to the cemetery. At the graveside Théodore de Banville gave the funeral oration, in which he acclaimed *Les Fleurs du mal* the work of a genius—a work "essentially French, essentially original, and essentially new."

Banville was followed by Asselineau who, fighting back the tears, attempted to dispel the legend that had hidden the real Baudelaire: "His sincere and delicate spirit possessed the modesty of his virtues and, through horror of affectation and hypocrisy, seized upon an ironic reserve that, in his case, was only a supreme form of dignity. I can only pity those who were deceived by it," he added.[19]

As he spoke, the gentle autumn rain grew heavier, silencing the speaker and dispersing the crowd. Baudelaire was once again alone, "far from the scoffing world, far from the dissolute crowd," as he had once written in his poem, "A une Martyre." It was for posterity to discover the indisputable truth of Banville's pronouncement: "The author of *Les Fleurs du mal* is not a poet of talent, but a poet of genius."[20]

Chapter Two
His Aesthetic Ideas

Le Salon de 1845

Because of Baudelaire's firm belief in the unity of the arts, his aesthetic ideas are scattered throughout his various essays, whether on art, poetry, or music. Moreover, what he says of one art form often applies to another. Thus in *Le Salon de 1845,* in which he urges artists to exploit the beauty of modern life, as proof of the validity of his argument, he cites not an artist, but the great novelist Balzac. Likewise, to understand fully Baudelaire's ideas on literature as well as on art, it is essential to read in his *Salon de 1859* what he has to say about the role of the imagination. The genesis of that idea, in turn, may be found in his essay on Poe.

In his first important publication, *Le Salon de 1845,* Baudelaire was following a century-old tradition that had had its finest expression in the *Salons* of Diderot, the great eighteenth-century critic, whose easy conversational tone is clearly reflected in the style of both *Le Salon de 1845* and *Le Salon de 1846.*

The chief interest of *Le Salon de 1845* lies in Baudelaire's recognition of Delacroix "as the most original painter of ancient or modern times" (*OC,* 2:353). One of the first to recognize the genius of the great Romantic artist, he continued throughout his life to praise and defend his work.

Equally important in *Le Salon de 1845* is Baudelaire's ringing affirmation that art should seek its inspiration in contemporary life: "No one is heeding tomorrow's wind, and yet the heroism of *modern life* surrounds us and crowds in upon us. . . . The *painter,* the true painter will be he who can seize the epic character of contemporary life and make us see and understand, through color or design, how great and poetic we are in our cravats and our patent leather boots" (*OC,* 2:407). Baudelaire never abandoned this concern for modernity in art. It was the source of some of his finest poetic inspiration, and one of his most famous essays, *Le Peintre de la vie moderne,* proved to be a glorification of the artistic and literary potential of contemporary life.

For some reason Baudelaire was so dissatisfied with *Le Salon de 1845* that he destroyed all the unsold copies. Champfleury suggests that Baudelaire may have been distressed by its lack of individuality and by what he owed, both in style and ideas, to Diderot, Heine, and Stendhal, and there is no doubt that it lacks the originality that will mark his future criticism. But even more important, the poet-critic may have been concerned by a contradiction that seems to invalidate his arguments: namely that Delacroix, whose genius he extols, was far from being the "true painter" who finds his inspiration in the life around him. Delacroix's paintings are markedly lacking in "cravats and patent leather boots." Baudelaire found himself in a dilemma that he would try to resolve in *Le Salon de 1846,* for he was never to relinquish his admiration for Delacroix or to renounce his belief that modern art should find its inspiration in modern life.

Deroy's influence may help to explain the praise evidenced by both Baudelaire and Asselineau for the mediocre allegorical painting *The Fountain of Youth* by William Haussoullier, a fellow student of Deroy in the atelier of Paul Delaroche.[1] In fairness to Baudelaire, however, it must be admitted that his praise is tempered by important reservations that are skillfully and subtly introduced: Haussoullier's use of color, though "distinguished," is of "a terrible and unrelenting rawness"; the artist may one day become "a genuine colorist." Moreover, in the last paragraph Baudelaire hints that Haussoullier may know "a little *too much* [italics added] about the work of certain Venetian painters. That is a truly dangerous scourge, and one that represses the spontaneity of many an excellent impulse. Let him beware of his erudition, let him beware even of his taste" (*OC,* 2:407). There seems little doubt that Baudelaire had noted both the lack of originality and a certain lack of taste in the artist's use of color.

Le Salon de 1846

In *Le Salon de 1846* Baudelaire returns to the question of Delacroix's modernity by emphasizing his Romanticism, which he considered a form of modern art: "Romanticism is precisely situated neither in the choice of subject nor in exact truth, but in a manner of feeling. . . . To say Romanticism is to say modern art" (*OC,* 2:420, 421).

Baudelaire's insistence that Delacroix's use of melancholy made him the "true painter of the nineteenth century" seems somewhat inconsistent with a previous claim that the true artist would be he who sought modernity through choice of subject. Obviously, the poet-critic had come to believe that modernity could be attained in more than one way: Balzac had found it in his choice of subject, in his treatment of the problems of contemporary society; Delacroix found it in his manner of feeling, in his depiction of universal and timeless emotions through the use of color and contour.

And so in 1846, Baudelaire begins his chapter on Delacroix by viewing him as the head of the modern school: "Romanticism and color lead me straight to Eugène Delacroix. I do not know if he is proud of being designated Romantic; but his place is here, because for a long time—from his first work, in fact—the majority of the public has viewed him as the head of the *modern* school" (*OC*, 2:421).

In contrast to the conventional format of *Le Salon de 1845,* in which paintings were discussed according to genres and each artist was evaluated in one or more paragraphs, *Le Salon de 1846* reveals a Baudelaire who breaks with tradition and subordinates the criticism of individual artists and their works to a provocative discussion of aesthetic ideas that, in many respects, are as pertinent to literature as they are to the visual arts. Thematic comments alternate with analysis and description, a method he will henceforth follow in his critical writings. As in *Le Salon de 1845,* he borrows— sometimes extensively—from Diderot, Heine, and Stendhal; yet like Samuel Cramer in *La Fanfarlo,* he succeeds, despite his imitative faculty, in remaining original.

The first problem that Baudelaire poses in *Le Salon de 1846* pertains to the nature of criticism. "I sincerely believe," he writes, "that the best criticism is that which is amusing and poetic; not a cold, mathematical criticism that, under the pretext of explaining everything, shows neither hate nor love, and deliberately rids itself of every vestige of temperament" (*OC*, 2:418). From the outset, then, it is clear that, according to Baudelaire, criticism should be intensely personal, and that the critic's task is neither to display his own erudition nor to remain impassive. On the contrary, the critic should freely reveal the pleasure or displeasure he feels in the presence of a work of art.

Moreover, it is the task of the critic to subject himself to the vision of the artist, to feel the experience that the artist has sought to express, and then to "reflect" that experience through his own temperament: "Since a beautiful picture is nature reflected by an artist, the best criticism will be the reflection of that picture by an intelligent and sensitive mind."[2] Such being the case, the best criticism of a picture could well be a sonnet or an elegy, Baudelaire reminds us, half in jest. The reader has only to remember a poem like "Les Phares" ("Beacons") to appreciate his remark. Such criticism, he freely admits, however, is "destined for anthologies" (*OC*, 2:418). "Criticism properly speaking," the poet-critic continues, "is justified only if it is biased, impassive, partisan, that is to say written from an exclusive point of view, but from a point of view that opens up the widest horizons" (*OC,* 2:418).

The Role of the Critic

To succeed in his purpose, Baudelaire was to insist many years later (in 1861) that the critic must possess the ability to recognize the "individualism" or the "temperament" of the artist: "An artist must possess something essentially *sui generis* by virtue of which he is *he* and not another" (*OC,* 2:806). In other words, the artist must be able to discover the particular beauty that distinguishes that artist from all others.

In his essay on the Exposition of 1855, Baudelaire frankly admits the impossibility of adhering to any preconceived system or fixed criteria: "More than once I have tried . . . to confine myself within a system in order to preach freely. But a system is a kind of damnation which forces us into a perpetual recantation; it is always necessary to invent another. . . . Constantly condemned to the humiliation of a new conversion, I made an important decision. To escape the horror of these philosophical apostasies, I proudly resigned myself to modesty: I was *content to feel*" (*OC,* 2:577–78; italics added).

Yet whether he realized it or not, Baudelaire was indeed following a system, the first step of which he had described in 1846 and which he reiterated in 1855: "I was content to feel." In other words, he had been attempting to sense the artistic experience and to reflect or re-create it for the reader. At the same time, consciously or unconsciously, he was endeavoring to discover "the mysterious intentions and the method" that lay behind the work in question. It was not until his 1861 essay on Wagner that he acknowledges his efforts "to penetrate more deeply into the understanding of those singular works . . . to discover the why and wherefore, and to transform pleasure into knowledge. . . ." (*OC,* 2:786).

The "system" Baudelaire had unwittingly found revealed both his superb poetic imagination and his keen analytical mind. And so the question "What is the good of criticism?" asked by him in 1846 was not fully answered until 1861. Only then did he realize that his criticism was not only the "reflection" of the beauty contained in a work of art, but also the analysis and generalization of the laws that govern artistic phenomena and that permit him to "transform pleasure into knowledge."

Beauty—the Goal of Art

For Baudelaire the goal of all the arts was beauty—an idea he was never to relinquish except during a brief period when he was attracted to a more utilitarian concept of art.[3] It was in *Le Salon de 1846* that he first stated unequivocally his belief that "the arts . . . are always the expression of the beautiful through the feeling, the passion, and the dreams of each man, that is to say a variety within a unity. . . ." (*OC*, 2:418). In other words, in addition to its absolute or eternal aspects, beauty also possesses a variable or particular aspect that is determined by the temperament or sensibility of the artist in question. It is here that Baudelaire breaks with the prevailing thought of the day, namely, that beauty is absolute and that it is created by strict adherence to academic rules laid down by pundits in accord with their study of the past.

At the end of *Le Salon de 1846,* Baudelaire, reiterating his concept of beauty, stresses the two components that it contains: "All forms of beauty . . . contain something eternal and something transitory—something absolute and something particular. Absolute or eternal beauty does not exist, or rather it is only an abstraction skimmed from the surface of a variety of beauties. The particular element in each manifestation comes from the emotions and just as we have our own particular emotions, so we have our own beauty" (*OC*, 2:493). In other words, particular beauty is determined by the temperament of the artist and by the character of the epoch in question, or, as he writes in *Le Peintre de la vie moderne,* by "the age, its fashions, its morals, its emotions" (*OC*, 2:685).

Baudelaire's concept of beauty explains the scorn for the neoclassicism of the Pagan School he expressed in his essay of 1852. In reproducing only the eternal element found in the past and by neglecting the circumstantial elements that characterize the present, the Pagan School had forfeited all claims to originality, he maintained. Its adherents had failed to realize, as Baudelaire was to write in *Le Peintre de la vie moderne,* that "almost all our originality comes from the stamp that *time* imprints upon our feelings" (*OC*, 2:696).

Modernity in Art

Baudelaire's belief in the particular aspect of beauty is also closely related to his idea of modernity: "Modernity is the half of art, of which the other half is the eternal and the immutable" (*OC*, 2:695). It is to be found everywhere, though nowhere more often than in the city—"in the spectacle of fashionable life and the thousands of stray souls—criminals and kept women—who drift about in the underground of a great city. . . ." (*OC,* 2:495). Balzac had discovered in the life of the city this aspect of particular beauty; Baudelaire himself did likewise in *La Fanfarlo,* the "Tableaux parisiens" of *Les Fleurs du mal,* and the *Petits Poèmes en prose.* Like Balzac, he had found in the life of a city, "so rich in poetic and marvelous subjects," the particular element of beauty that was being neglected by the artists and writers of his day.

Because of the importance Baudelaire assigns to the epic possibilities of contemporary life, heroism becomes one of the key words in his essays. As early as 1845, he had encouraged the true painter "to seize the epic character of contemporary life," and in 1846 he renews his appeal to artists to seek the beauty and the heroism of modern life (*OC,* 2:407).

Equally important as the epic or heroic character of modern life was his emphasis on the mysterious beauty to be found in the teeming life of the city: "Parisian life is rich in poetic and marvelous subjects. The marvelous envelops and penetrates us like the atmosphere itself, but we do not see it" (*OC,* 2:496). Because Baudelaire had so often detected it in the life around him, he could say to the city of Paris in his unfinished epilogue to *Les Fleurs du mal:* "You have given me your mud, and I have turned it into gold" (*OC,* 1:192).

There were a few others who, like Baudelaire, had also succeeded in discovering the marvelous and the poetic, Guys, Méryon, Daumier, and Balzac among them. Méryon's art, in fact, often seems a visual equivalent of Baudelaire's *Tableaux parisiens* and even of certain of his prose poems. Artist and poet alike sometimes give an almost demonic significance to the commonplace: Baudelaire in the sinister images of his two poems "Le Crépuscule du matin" ("Dawn") and "Le Crépuscule du soir" ("Twilight") —"demons bumping against shutters, the lamp like a bloody palpitating eye," Méryon in his portrayal of the black ominous birds filling the Parisian sky or of other strange and irrational elements that appear in his etchings.[4]

That Baudelaire chose Guys rather than Daumier or Manet for his long and remarkable essay "The Painter of Modern Life" (written between 1859 and 1860 and published as late as 1863) has often been cited as a mistake in judgment. However, Baudelaire discovered in his sketches and watercolors the modernity he found so lacking in the visual art of his contemporaries.

Given Baudelaire's enthusiasm for Daumier, it seems strange that he failed to write elsewhere about his extraordinary genius. Evidently he had done so at one point, for in his correspondence he alludes to a laudatory article on the artist that the editor Martinet had rejected and lost, despite Baudelaire's warning that he had failed to make a copy.[5] Moreover one of his last poems, written in Brussels, praised the genius of Daumier who, he claimed, "in painting Evil and its sequel . . . proves the beauty of his heart."

At the time that Baudelaire wrote *The Painter of Modern Life,* Manet would not have been suitable as the subject of his essay. Before his departure for Brussels, Baudelaire had seen only a few of Manet's paintings, most of which were markedly lacking in the modernity that was to characterize his later work. Moreover, there is little doubt that it was largely the influence of Baudelaire that later prompted the abrupt change in Manet's style from what Nils Sandblat calls "his paraphrases of Rubens and Velasquez to the realism of the *flaneur.*"[6]

Although Antonin Proust, Manet's friend from childhood, maintains that it was the artist who influenced the poet—and to a certain extent he was right—the opposite seems even more true. Nowhere is Baudelaire's influence more obvious than in Manet's painting *Olympia.* The composition of the picture was borrowed from Titian, but the flavor or tone was distinctly Baudelairean. Wearing only a bracelet, earrings, a black ribbon around her throat, a flower in her hair, and slippers on her feet, Olympia calls to mind the woman celebrated by Baudelaire in his poem "Les Bijoux" ("Jewels"): "La très chère était nue, et, connaissant mon coeur / Elle n'avait gardé que ses bijoux sonores" ("My beloved was naked, and knowing my heart / She had kept on only her sonorous jewels").

But it is not only the ornaments worn by Olympia that remind us of "Les Bijoux." Certain phrases of the poem—"the triumphant air," "the boyish bosom," "her eyes fixed on me like a tamed tigress"—seem as true of Olympia as of Baudelaire's courtesan.

Equally Baudelairean in character are the Negress holding a bouquet of flowers and the little black cat, reminiscent of the cats that prowl through Baudelaire's work that aroused a furor on the part of the public, who attributed to them an almost diabolic significance.

The Nature of Beauty

In Baudelaire's eyes, "*the beautiful is always strange.* I do not mean that it is deliberately or coldly strange," he wrote in *L'Exposition universelle de 1855.* "I mean that it always contains a bit of strangeness, an artless, unpremeditated, unconscious strangeness. . . . Reverse the proposition and try to imagine a commonplace beauty" (*OC,* 1:578). Like Poe, who quoted Bacon's famous dictum, "There is no exquisite beauty without some strangeness in its proportions," he too believed that the strange or the "bizarre," as he liked to call it, is the "indispensable condiment" of all beauty (*OC,* 1:579). Baudelaire's emphasis on the strange has nothing to do with its shock value, but is rather a way of protesting against the commonplace and the banal. Like modernity it is a necessary ingredient of variable beauty, since, as the poet suggests, it is determined by "climate, milieu, race, religion, custom, and the artist's temperament" (*OC,* 1:578).

Melancholy and horror are also associated with beauty: "It is one of the astounding prerogatives of art that the horrible, artistically expressed, becomes beauty, and that *sorrow,* when given rhythm and cadence, fills the heart with a serene *joy*" (*OC,* 2:123). In poems like "Hymne à la beauté," "Une Charogne," and "Une Martyre," the poet himself has attempted to transform horror into beauty, whereas in the lovely "Recueillement," with its evocation of the slow, heavy coming of the night, he has succeeded brilliantly in giving sorrow a rhythm and cadence that despite the overtone of deep sadness "fills the mind with serene joy."

Baudelaire's Conception of Beauty

In his *Journaux intimes* Baudelaire describes his *own* conception of particular beauty at length. For him, beauty is first of all "something ardent and sad, something slightly vague that allows for conjecture" (*OC,* 1:657–58). In other words, like all the Romanticists, he insists on the inseparability of pleasure and pain. We have only to think of Shelley ("the sweetest songs are those that tell of saddest thoughts"), Alfred de Musset ("the most despairing are the most beautiful of songs"), or Poe ("a certain taint of sadness is inseparably connected with all the higher manifestations of beauty") to see how close he was to the Romanticists in associating beauty with sadness. But whereas pain for the Romanticists usually took the form of the *mal du siècle* and was often no more than a pose, in the case of Baudelaire pain assumes the quality of spleen and tends to be more pathological in nature.

In the "something slightly vague that allows room for conjecture," Baudelaire can be said to be anticipating Symbolism. In his essay on Wagner he expresses much the same idea: "In music, as in painting and even in the *written word,* which is nevertheless the most positive of the arts, there is always a lacuna completed by the imagination of the listener" (*OC,* 2:781–82). Many years later, Mallarmé was to make a similar observation in his pronouncement that for him a poem was "a mystery whose key the reader must seek."[7]

Other components that constitute Baudelaire's *own* conception of par-

ticular beauty are mystery, which he considers one of the most interesting
characteristics of beauty and which he will praise in the poetry of Victor
Hugo; regret, a theme that occurs again and again in his own poetry; and
unhappiness or melancholy that in contrast to joy—"one of the more commonplace ornaments" of poetry—is in his opinion indispensable to poetry
(*OC*, 1:659).

    After thus analyzing his own view of poetry, Baudelaire's conclusion is at
first glance surprising: "Sustained—others might say obsessed—by these
ideas, it is understandable that it would be difficult for me not to conclude
that the most perfect type of masculine Beauty is *Satan*—as Milton conceived him" (*OC*, 1:658). Seen in the light of Romanticism, there is nothing
particularly new or sensational about his admission. The Romanticists had
long admired Milton's conception of Lucifer, for, as Mario Praz has observed, Milton had given to Lucifer "the charm of an untamed rebel . . . an
aspect of fallen beauty, of splendor shadowed by sadness and death; he is
majestic though in ruins."[8] Shelley maintained that "nothing can exceed the
energy and magnificence of the character of Satan as expressed in *Paradise
Lost*"; Chateaubriand insisted that Satan was "one of the most sublime and
pathetic conceptions ever conceived by a poet"; de Vigny intended to write
an epic poem called "Satan Sauvé"; Hugo who borrowed that idea, portrays
the reconciliation of God and Satan in "La Fin de Satan."

    In this extended definition of beauty—*his own* conception of beauty—
Baudelaire makes only a passing reference to its spiritual aspects. In his
1857 essay on Poe, however, he agrees with the American poet that "the
principle of poetry is, precisely and simply, human aspiration toward a supe-
rior beauty," and he comes to see in both poetry and music a means of
attaining the infinite and of glimpsing "the splendors beyond the tomb"
(*OC*, 2:334).

Baudelaire and Realism

    Convinced that beauty was the goal of all art, Baudelaire was naturally
concerned with the means by which it could be sought. He soon came to
distrust the direct imitation of nature. Realism, "that silly cult of nature, un-
touched by the imagination" became abhorrent to him, whether it was in
painting, in literature, or photography (*OC*, 2:660).

    Although for a short time (ca. 1844–50) he had shown a modicum of
interest in the Realist movement and had been attracted by the ideas prom-
ulgated by his friends Champfleury, Courbet, and Proudhon, Baudelaire
soon broke "with that rabble of vulgar artists and writers whose myopic in-

telligence takes refuge behind the vague and obscure term known as *realism*" (*OC*, 2:747). Like Flaubert, he objected to having his art characterized as realism. To him it was "a disgusting insult flung in the face of all analysts, a vague and elastic word which, for the rabble, means not a new method of creation, but a minute description of details" (*OC*, 2:80).

In *Le Salon de 1859*, Baudelaire explains his reasons for his dislike of Realism: "I find it useless and irksome to represent what exists, because nothing that exists satisfies me. Nature is ugly and I prefer the monsters of my fantasy to positive triviality" (*OC*, 2:6). A definition of poetry, contained among the notes for an 1855 article that he had evidently intended as an indictment of Realism, shows how far he had moved from the thinking of his former friends and associates: "Poetry is what is most real, what is completely true only *in another world*. This world [is] a hieroglyphic dictionary" (*OC*, 2:59). The definition clearly reveals the influence of both Poe and Delacroix.

From this moment on, Baudelaire became even more convinced of the aesthetic dangers of direct imitation of nature. In *Le Salon de 1859*, he warns both artists and writers:

In recent years we have heard it said in a thousand different ways: "copy nature, copy only nature. There is no finer triumph than an excellent copy of nature." And this doctrine, so inimical to art, was alleged to apply not only to painting, but to all the arts, even to the novel, even to poetry. To these doctrinaires, so satisfied with nature, an imaginative man would certainly have had the right to answer: "I find it useless and tiresome to portray things as they are, because nothing that exists satisfies me. Nature is ugly, and I prefer the monsters of my imagination to the triteness of actuality." (*OC*, 2:619–20)

But Baudelaire will not completely reject nature. Adopting Delacroix's observation that nature is only a dictionary, he goes on to say: Painters who obey their imagination seek in their dictionaries the elements which fit their conception. . . . Those who lack imagination copy the dictionary. The result is a very great vice, the vice of banality" (*OC*, 2:624–25).

The Role of the Imagination

The interpretation of this "hieroglyphic dictionary" becomes, then, the major problem of the artist. To intensify their sense of perception, many artists, including Baudelaire himself, resorted to artificial means such as drugs and alcohol. Baudelaire early recognized the perils of "this dangerous road," and in the *Paradis artificiels* as well as in a letter to Armand Fraisse of 12 August 1860 warned against the risks that lie ahead.

It is imagination, "the queen of faculties," that alone can aid the poet or artist in conquering nature and discovering true reality. "The whole visible universe is only a storehouse of images and signs to which the imagination will give a place and a relative value; it is a sort of food which the imagination must digest and transform," he writes in *Le Salon de 1859* (*OC*, 2:627).

But imagination is not sufficient in itself. It must be aided by reverie, contemplation, and dream—key words that appear time and again in Baudelaire's writings. The faculty of reverie, it should be added, is not simply a matter of daydreaming. On the contrary, in *Les Paradis artificiels,* the poet-critic maintains that it is "a divine and mysterious faculty; for it is in dreams that man communicates with the shadowy world that surrounds him" (*OC*, 2:497). It was through revery and contemplation that Delacroix, aided by imagination, had succeeded in translating "the invisible, the impalpable, the dream" (*OC*, 2:744).

The Role of Memory

Equally important in helping the imagination pursue its vision of beauty and interpret the mysteries of the universe is the role of memory. For Baudelaire, memory serves as a sort of catalytic agent that helps the artist to distinguish between trivial detail and essential facts.

Studies of landscapes, improvised in front of sea and sky, by the artist Boudin, were in Baudelaire's opinion comparable to taking notes. It was in the artist's *studio* that his imagination, aided by memory, transformed those studies into works of art. Even more significant is the role of memory in stimulating the imagination to recall the distant past. In his second essay on Poe, he maintained that the deliberate recall of sensory impressions, such as perfumes and sounds, enable the poet to re-create or recover the past. It was, in fact, exercising this deliberate recall that enabled him in "Parfum Exotique" (1857) to see ports filled with sails and masts, to hear the song of the sailors, and to glimpse the white-capped waves of tropical seas dancing under the dazzling fires of "monotonous suns"—memories of his aborted voyage to India.

Marcel Proust, a great admirer of Baudelaire, was fascinated by the relationship between his own conception of memory and that of the poet. For Proust, memory must be involuntary if it is to be creative. For Baudelaire, imagination alone is creative; memory is but its handmaiden. In *Les Paradis artificiels,* Baudelaire maintains that childhood memories contain "the germ of the artist's strange reveries, or better still, of his genius" (*OC,* 1:497). In *Le Peintre de la vie moderne,* he returns to this idea and boldly declares that "genius is only *childhood recovered* at will, childhood now endowed, in order to express itself, with virile organs and with an analytical mind that enables it to order and arrange all the materials accumulated involuntarily" (*OC,* 2:690).

Throughout Baudelaire's life, then, a work of art—a picture, a poem, or a novel—continues to be what it had been in 1846: "nature reflected by an artist." The artist's vision of beauty is inspired by contemplation and memory and transformed by imagination and proper technique into a work of art.

Correspondence

Of all the functions of the imagination, the most important, Baudelaire believed, is its ability to perceive correspondences. Writing to Toussenel in 1856, he describes imagination as "the most *scientific* of the faculties because it alone understands *universal analogy* or what a mystic religion calls *correspondence*" (*Corr.,* 1:336). A year later he reaffirms this belief in his essay on Poe: "Imagination is an almost divine faculty that perceives immediately and without philosophic methods the inner and secret relations of things, the correspondences, and the analogies" (*OC,* 2:328).

Like Mme de Staël, Sainte-Beuve, and Nerval, among others, he believes that correspondences may be either synesthetic or transcendental, horizontal or vertical. Synesthetic correspondences and analogies are, in his opinion, almost inescapable: "What would be really surprising would be that sound *could not* suggest color, that colors *could not* convey a melody, and that sound and color were unsuited to translating ideas, things always having been expressed by a reciprocal analogy since the day when God created the world as a complex and indivisible whole" (*OC,* 2:784).

But even more important theoretically than the synesthetic correspondences are the transcendental correspondences that exist between the visible and the invisible worlds. Influenced mainly by Swedenborg and Fourier, Baudelaire accepts an age-old doctrine, both pagan and Christian, that sees in nature "a forest of symbols" and views "the earth and its spectacles as a revelation, as something in *correspondence with Heaven*" (*OC,* 2:113–14). Since, as Baudelaire writes in his essay on Hugo, "everything is hieroglyphic," the poet becomes a "translator, a decipherer" who finds in the universe "a vast storehouse of images and signs that must be digested and transformed" (*OC*, 2:133).

Despite what Baudelaire writes in his essays about the use of symbolism in *Les Fleurs de mal,* he tends to replace the traditional "symbolique" with a personal symbolism, as Lloyd Austin points out in his penetrating analysis of Baudelaire's technique.[9] On the other hand, the poet's imagination seldom takes us out of the world below; rather, it establishes a relationship between nature and the inner world of the poet through the use of symbols that give concrete form to inner experiences or ideas. Thus Robert Vivier is quite right in describing the doctrine of universal analogies professed by Baudelaire as a sort of "aesthetician's myth."[10]

Baudelaire's conception of the imagination owes little or nothing to Poe or to Coleridge, as is sometimes believed. It is true he found the confirmation of the idea in Poe, but as early as 1846 he had indirectly exalted the imagination by assigning a preeminent role to the artist's temperament and by insisting that "the first task of the artist is to substitute man for nature and to protest against nature" (*OC*, 2:473). There is no evidence that Baudelaire had even read Coleridge; it is generally conceded that he only knew the English writer's ideas indirectly through the works of Poe and through Mrs. Crowe, whom he cites in *Le Salon de 1859.*

On the other hand, Delacroix, whom Baudelaire had met in 1845, did much to shape the poet's conception of the imagination. On several occasions the poet-critic cites Delacroix's observation that nature is only a dictionary and in 1859 uses this metaphor to develop his theory of the imagination. In a final, warm tribute written after the artist's death in 1863, Baudelaire emphasizes once again the fact that, in Delacroix's eyes, imagination was the most precious of gifts and the most important of faculties.

The Importance of Technique

Valuable as the role of the imagination was to Baudelaire, he believed, like Daumier, that imagination "remained impotent and sterile if it did not have at its command a rapid skill that could follow the great, despotic faculty in all its impatient whims" (*OC*, 2:747). From his early essays Baudelaire had insisted on the necessity of subjecting imagination and inspiration to discipline. In 1846 he had warned that the artist's "naïveté and temperament should be aided by all the means that technique provides" (*OC*, 2:419). In *Le Salon de 1859* he is even more explicit: "The more imagination one has, the more necessary it is to possess a technique that will accompany it in its adventures and overcome the difficulties it eagerly seeks out" (*OC,* 2:612).

Baudelaire himself followed his own advice and reworked his poems with painstaking care. He was not a facile creator of images and rhymes, as he explained to his mother: "I don't know how many times you have spoken to me about *my facility,*" he wrote her in February 1865. "Facility in conception or facility in expression? I have never had either one or the other, and it must be quite obvious that the little I have done is the result of very painful effort" (*Corr.,* 2:450).

It was this desire for perfection of form, in addition to his mastery of expression, that explains much of the greatness of *Les Fleurs du mal.* Had the expression been weak or banal, the reader would have been less moved by the anguish and despair, the sensual joys and spiritual needs that he voices in his greatest and most haunting poems. Baudelaire was never to forget that "idea and form are two beings in one" and that to neglect form is "to destroy poetry" (*OC,* 2:143).

Art and Morality

The question of the relationship of art and morality was one that deeply concerned Baudelaire throughout his life. Early poems, like "J'aime le souvenir" or "La Muse malade," written early in his career, reveal the influence of the neoclassicists, especially Banville and Nerval. For a short time, however, Baudelaire was to renounce the ideas of the classical revival and to adopt a more utilitarian conception of art inspired by the 1848 Revolution and by his association with Proudhon and Pierre Dupont. Early memories of the industrial strife and of the misery of the working class that he had witnessed during his school days in Lyons all contributed to his change of attitude. In fact, in an essay written in 1851 on the rather mediocre poetry of Dupont, he actually denounced the "puerile Utopia of the school of *art for art's sake*" and boldly proclaimed that "art should be inseparable from morality and utility" (*OC,* 2:26, 27). In another article written at about the same time, he strongly condemned the "Pagan School" for its rejection of reason and passion and maintained unreservedly that "literature must walk hand in hand with science and philosophy" (*OC,* 2:45).

It was not long, however, before Baudelaire realized that he had gone too far; he came to see that the relationship of morality to art was not as direct as he had maintained. Thus, in *Les Drames et les romans honnêtes* the poet-critic modified his opinion, adopting a view that was never to change. "Art is useful," he wrote, "because it is art; pernicious art," he continued, "is that which distorts the conditions of life" (*OC,* 2:41).

This return to a more aristocratic conception of art was undoubtedly influenced, in part at least, by Baudelaire's discovery of Poe and Joseph de Maistre. Though he fully agreed with the American poet that utility was "the great heresy of modern times," he does not go as far as Poe in maintaining that art and morality must be completely divorced from each other. On the contrary, he acknowledges that a certain morality is *implicit* in all great art. And so in his review of *Madame Bovary* he maintains that "the logic of the work satisfies all the claims of morality, and that it is for the reader to draw his conclusions from the conclusion" (*OC,* 2:82). Likewise, he admires the implicit moralizing of Hugo, but despises the explicit moralizing that is to be found in *Les Misérables.*

Baudelaire makes himself most clear on the relation of art to morality in a letter written a few years before his death to the English poet Algernon Swinburne: "I am not so much a *moralist* as you obligingly pretend to think. I simply believe (as you do, no doubt) that every poem, every work of art that is *well done,* inevitably and necessarily suggests *a moral.* It is up to the reader. I even have a very decided dislike for any exclusively moral intention in a poem" (*Corr.,* 2:325).[11]

The Nature and Function of Poetry

Though Baudelaire failed to write an essay devoted to his personal conception of the nature and function of poetry, it is clear from one particular draft of a preface to *Les Fleurs du mal* that at one time he had intended to answer the question "What is poetry?" Evidently he abandoned the idea, discouraged by the hopelessness of his task: "I was stopped by the appalling futility of explaining anything to anyone."[12] However, a number of provocative statements found throughout his writings reveal his ideas on poetry in general and on his own poetry in particular. In a letter to Armand Fraisse of 18 February 1860, in which he criticizes the poetry of Alfred de Musset, he accuses Musset of never being able "to understand the work through which a reverie is transformed into art" (*Corr.,* 1:675). Baudelaire's use of the word *reverie* clearly indicates that for him poetry is above all the poet's own inner world, externalized and perfected in form by the use of a technique that is perfectly adapted to the subject.

Elsewhere, Baudelaire stresses the spiritual aspect of poetry. Two years later, in his 1857 essay on Poe, he emphasizes its ability to reveal the beauty and mystery of the invisible world: "It is at the same time by poetry and *through* poetry, by and *through* music that the soul glimpses the splendors beyond the tomb, and when an exquisite poem brings us to the verge of tears, those tears are not the proof of excessive pleasure; they are rather evidence of an aroused melancholy, of a condition of nerves, of a nature that has been exiled amid the imperfect and which would like to take possession immediately, on this very earth, of a revealed paradise" (*OC*, 2:334).

In his essay on Banville, Baudelaire characterizes poetry in a way that is far more reminiscent of much of his own verse: "Every lyric poet by virtue of his nature inevitably effects a return to the lost Eden" (*OC*, 2:165). We have only to think of the poems in which he returns to the lost Eden of his childhood, of tropical seas and skies, or of happiness he had once known, to realize how, through imagination and reverie, he had recaptured an idealized past and restored it to the present.

But it is in the opening lines of his short essay *L'Art philosophique* that Baudelaire best explains his conception of poetry and of art in general: "What is the modern conception of pure art? It is to create a suggestive magic containing both the object and the subject, the world outside the artist and the artist himself" (*OC*, 2:598). This superb formula characterizes much of Baudelaire's greatest verse and became the basis of the poetic theory of the Symbolists.

Chapter Three

Critic of Contemporary Literature

There has long been a tendency to separate Baudelaire's criticism of art from his writings on literature and to maintain the superiority of the former over the latter. The fact that Eugène Crépet commissioned him to write on ten of his contemporaries, including such mediocre writers as Jules Janin and Hégésippe Moreau, has done much to foster this belief. Yet it must be admitted that to divorce his art criticism from his literary criticism is to deny their fundamental unity and to ignore Baudelaire's belief that all the arts—especially poetry, music, and painting—are interrelated. Moreover, it is important to note that in his essays Baudelaire shows himself aware of both the faults and merits of the authors in question and that he did not hesitate to express in the harshest terms his distaste for mediocrity. In fact, his criticism of Hégésippe Moreau was so devastating that it proved unacceptable and was rejected both by Crépet and by Catulle Mendès, editor of *La Revue fantaisiste*. Even when it finally appeared in the 1868 posthumous edition of Baudelaire's writings it provoked unfavorable comment, although Moreau had been dead for thirty years.

In a letter to Ancelle, dated 18 February 1866, Baudelaire reveals with remarkable acuity of judgment those writers among his contemporaries whom he considers truly great: "Except for Chateaubriand, Balzac, Stendhal, Mérimée, de Vigny, Flaubert, Banville, Gautier, and Leconte de Lisle, all of the modern rabble are obnoxious to me" (*OC,* 2:61). Of these, he has written articles on Flaubert, Banville, Gautier, and Leconte de Lisle. It is known that he admired Chateaubriand enormously and had intended to defend him against the attacks of Villemain, for he saw in the author of *René* the creator of "the great school of melancholy" as well as "the father of dandyism"—a great compliment coming from Baudelaire.

Baudelaire's references to Balzac prove that he understood his genius better than Sainte-Beuve and other critics of his time. In fact, the page that Baudelaire devoted to Balzac in his essay on Gautier proved to be so perceptive that it has become one of the principle sources of Balzacian criticism. It is this page, in fact, that inspired Albert Béguin to write his *Balzac visionnaire*.

That Baudelaire did not devote a critical essay to Alfred de Vigny is somewhat surprising, since in his 1859 essay on Gautier he had written: "Victor Hugo, Sainte-Beuve, and Alfred de Vigny rejuvenated, or better still renewed, French poetry, dead since the time of Corneille" (*OC*, 2:110). Moreover, both Baudelaire and de Vigny had similar ideas pertaining to modern society and to progress, and both had exalted the role of the imagination in the creative arts.

Baudelaire's failure to write about Stendhal and Prosper Mérimée is equally disappointing. We know that he admired Mérimée personally and that he compared his manner and personality to that of Delacroix. Mérimée, on the other hand, dismissed *Les Fleurs du mal* as "mediocre and completely innocuous, showing only an occasional spark of poetry," and compared its author to a "poor, inexperienced boy weary of life because he has been deceived by a *grisette*."[1] Although Baudelaire says nothing of Stendhal's novels, he was obviously impressed by his critical views; there is no doubt that he borrowed heavily from him in formulating some of his own aesthetic ideas.

Baudelaire's writings reveal why, in his letter to Ancelle, he omitted the names of Lamartine and Musset. As a schoolboy, Baudelaire had read both poets with enthusiasm and had been especially influenced by the rich harmonies and gentle melancholy of the author of "le Lac." But in his 1852 essay on Poe he complains that both writers "lack willpower and are not sufficiently masters of themselves" (*OC*, 2:274). Some years later, in a letter to Armand Fraisse of 18 February 1860, he shows himself completely contemptuous of Musset's art: "I have never been able to endure that *paragon of lady killers,* his impudence of a spoiled child, invoking heaven and hell about hotel-room adventures, his muddy torrent of mistakes in grammar and prosody, and finally his utter incapacity to understand the work through which a reverie becomes a work of art" (*Corr.*, 1:675).

George Sand fares no better in Baudelaire's judgment of his contemporaries, for her moral, social, and political ideas were as obnoxious to him as her "famous *flowing style,* so dear to the bourgeoisie." It is especially in his *Journaux intimes* that he gives free vent to his contempt: "She is stupid, she is dull, she is garrulous. Her ideas on morality show the profundity of judgment and the delicacy of feeling of a concierge or a kept woman" (*OC*, 1:686). Elsewhere in the *Journaux* he writes: "she claims that a true Christian can not believe in Hell . . . she has good reason to wish to abolish Hell" (*OC*, 1:687). In fact, so violent was Baudelaire's reaction to "the

Prudhomme of immorality," as he called her, that had he chosen to write an article on Sand, it might well have been refused publication, as happened in the case of his essay on Hégésippe Moreau, commissioned by Eugène Crépet.

The name of Alexandre Dumas père does not appear among those Baudelaire listed in his letter of 30 March 1865 to Ancelle, but he readily admitted in a letter to Sainte-Beuve the fascination he first felt on reading Dumas' swashbuckling novels and dramas. Angered by the attitude of the Belgians toward the novelist, he protested their hypocrisy: "Even while forming a line to shake his hand, the Belgians made fun of him. That is disgraceful. A man may be respected for his *vitality*. The vitality of a Negro, to be sure. But I think that many others who, like me, are fond of the serious have been carried away by *La Dame de Montsoreau* and by *Balsamo*" (*Corr.*, 2:491).

What is truly surprising, however, is the omission of Victor Hugo's name among those mentioned to Ancelle. Baudelaire's attitude toward Hugo had always been somewhat ambivalent. In the *Salon de 1845* and that of *1846* he had disparaged the poet for his artificiality and for his pedantic use of symmetry and antithesis, faults that are more true of Hugo's early works where they are less often balanced out by his more solid virtues. Yet even in these earlier works, Baudelaire admits the "nobility" and the "majesty" that mark much of the work of his great contemporary and praises his admirable and curious dexterity in the use of his tools.

1859 seemed to mark a change in Baudelaire's view of Hugo's art, perhaps inspired in part by his hope of obtaining a letter-preface for his article on Gautier, which he was planning to republish in the form of a brochure. Yet, in all fairness to Baudelaire, it must be admitted that the publication of *Les Contemplations* (1856) and of *La Légende des siècles* (1859–63) had done much to change his opinion. The sincerity of his admiration for both works are confirmed by the comments made to his mother in a letter written in 1859: "I am very surprised by what you say about *La Légende des siècles.* . . . Hugo has never been so picturesque or so astonishing as at the beginning of *Rathbert* (Le Concile d'Ancône), *Zim-Zizimi, Le Mariage de Roland, La Rose de l'Infante;* they reveal dazzling powers which he alone possesses" (*Corr.*, 1:609).

It was Hugo's political and social ideas that exasperated and infuriated Baudelaire. His social and utilitarian ideas, his belief in progress, his conception of himself as "savior of the human race" were more than the poet-critic could bear. Moreover, Hugo's fame and fortune in contrast to his own poverty and ill health only increased the resentment and hostility he freely expressed in his correspondence and in his *Journaux intimes.*

Critics have long considered Baudelaire's 1862 essay on *Les Misérables* "réticent, voire perfide," as Crépet and Blin once characterized it; others, like Margaret Gilman, deplore its "sadly evasive conclusion" and its many "half-truths."[2] On close examination, however, it is obvious that the review is a brilliant tour de force in which Baudelaire could write an article seemingly favorable enough to be published in *Le Boulevard*—a paper strongly favoring Victor Hugo—while remaining entirely consistent with his own contrary aesthetic and philosophic ideas.[3]

Badly in need of money, unable to find a publisher, suffering from wretched health and from the torturing fear of losing his mind, Baudelaire resorted to a clever though somewhat devious method of writing a review of a book he heartily disliked but that he hoped would prove acceptable to a publisher (*OC,* 1:668).[4] The review begins with a long quotation from his 1861 article on Hugo in which he had sincerely praised the implicit, as opposed to the explicit, morality of *Les Contemplations* and *La Légende des siècles.* Without further comment, he adds in the most unequivocal manner: "Only one line needs to be added here, for in *Les Misérables* moralism does enter *directly*" [italics added] (*OC,* 2:218).

Quoting Hugo's own statement pertaining to the *utility* of the novel, Baudelaire heartily agrees and subtly praises Hugo's ability as a *propagandist* rather than as an artist. It should be remembered that Baudelaire detested utilitarian literature and had strongly condemned it in the past. Although he praises Hugo's characterization of Fantine, as well as his ability to portray childhood, he subtly discredits the validity of the novel by suggesting that Hugo uses false or specious arguments in order to build his thesis. Baudelaire concludes his article by an affirmation of his own belief in original sin and a sly dig at Hugo's inconsistency in maintaining the goodness of man while failing to accuse God of cruelty in allowing the innocent to suffer. With a final thrust at Hugo's belief in progress, he adds: "Alas, even after all the progress that we have been promised for so long, there will always remain sufficient traces of original sin to establish its everlasting reality!" (*OC,* 2:224).[5]

In his 1862 review, however, Baudelaire showed himself extraordinarily perceptive in discovering and defining the real greatness of Victor Hugo. Not only did he note his virtuosity, his universality, his phenomenal success in creating the modern epic, but, unlike other critics, he perceived Hugo's greatness as a metaphysical poet, his ability to express the mystery of life with the "indispensable obscurity" so essential to all great art, as well as the cosmic power, epic strength and sense of mystery that characterize his later work.

Equally surprising as his omission of Hugo's name in his letter to Ancelle in 1866, is Baudelaire's failure to include that of Sainte-Beuve. Perhaps no other writer had influenced him in his early youth as much as the author of *Volupté* and the *Poésies de Joseph Delorme*. In fact, their intimate psychological tone is often clearly reflected in *Les Fleurs du mal*. Baudelaire himself acknowledged his debt in an early mediocre poem and, as late as 1862, he still called himself "the incorrigible lover of *Rayons jaunes* and of *Volupté*." The relationship between the two men was always cordial, and Baudelaire seemed to remain genuinely fond of "l'oncle Beuve," despite the critic's failure ever to come to his defense.

Among the contemporary writers whose works Baudelaire admired in print were Flaubert, Banville, Gautier, and Leconte de Lisle. His analysis of the poetry of Leconte de Lisle remains one of the best ever made of the Parnassian poet. Baudelaire not only admired his highly disciplined art, his intellectual aristocracy, and his avoidance of Romantic sentimentality, but he also astutely recognized that the interest of the Creole poet in the pagan past was a means of escaping the transitory values of an age he despised and of evoking the immutable aspects of eternal nature.

Even more important was Baudelaire's recognition of the fact that the real originality of Leconte de Lisle lay in his portrayal of the "powerful, crushing forces of nature" and in his evocation of the primitive grandeur and the "majesty of animals in movement and repose." Baudelaire's judgment has long been confirmed by posterity and by later critics who agree with him that "in these respects, Leconte de Lisle is a master and a great master" (*OC,* 2:178).

Despite the differences between the poetry of Baudelaire and that of Banville, the author of *Les Fleurs du mal* never failed to appreciate the brilliant lyric talent of his friend's poetry.[6] Whereas writers like Maturin, Byron, Poe, and Baudelaire himself "cast resplendent, dazzling rays on the latent Lucifer hidden in every human heart," Banville, he maintained, was a "perfect classicist" in a "satanic and Romantic atmosphere" (*OC,* 2:168, 169). He had succeeded in effecting "a return to the lost Eden," as Baudelaire himself had done in some of his loveliest poems, and "to translate the beautiful hours of life, those hours when one feels happy to think and to be alive" (*OC,* 2:163, 165). Baudelaire's admiration for Banville remained unchanged until his death, as did that of the younger poet for the elder. Banville presented the moving funeral oration at Baudelaire's grave, and he also helped Asselineau prepare the posthumous edition of the poet-critic's works.

Of all the critical essays written by Baudelaire, that on *Madame Bovary* remains one of the most penetrating and insightful. Flaubert himself was delighted with the review and wrote to the poet: "Your article gave me the *greatest* pleasure. You entered into the arcana of the work as if my brains were yours. It is *deeply* understood and felt. If you find my book suggestive, I can only say that what you have written is no less so."[7]

Baudelaire recognized that Flaubert had put much of himself into the novel; in fact, Flaubert is said to have actually admitted, "Madame Bovary, c'est moi." Moreover, the poet-critic was especially impressed by the fact that Flaubert, unlike other Realists, had succeeded in transforming ugliness into beauty, and that he had proved—as had Baudelaire—that "all subjects are equally good or bad . . . that the most commonplace can become the best" (*OC,* 2:81).

Equally important in Baudelaire's eyes was the fact that Flaubert had refused to incorporate a moral indictment into his novel. Nowhere has he stated more clearly his view on the relationship of art and morality: "A true work of art need not contain an indictment. The logic of the work satisfies all the claims of morality, and it is for the reader to draw the conclusion from the conclusion" (*OC,* 2:81–82).

That Baudelaire considered Emma to be endowed with what he calls virile virtues—imagination, energy, dandyism, love of domination—is only properly understood if one realizes that he considered woman "a pure animal" completely devoid of these very characteristics. His *Journaux intimes* explains his viewpoint: In various notations he accuses women of being guided by sexual instinct or, as he says euphemistically in his review of *Madame Bovary,* by "what is *called* the *heart*" [italics added] (*OC,* 2:82). Woman, he insists, is "the contrary of the Dandy," who through the discipline of self-purification, can free himself from the natural life of the flesh and turn himself into a work of art (*OC,* 1:677).

Although Baudelaire's belief that imagination is strictly a virile quality is obviously mistaken, his assertion that Emma was guided by "the sophisms of her imagination" rather than by sexual instinct or physical desire is plainly true. A careful reading of the novel corroborates the fact that Emma, motivated by the reading of cheap romantic novels and by the power of her imagination, was led to pursue what she naively believed to be the ideal. Unlike his contemporary critics, Baudelaire also realized that the famous episode of the operation on Hippolyte's clubfoot and of Emma's interview with the inept priest were far from being extraneous. On the contrary, they only served to motivate her actions and to make her more an object of pity rather than condemnation.[8]

Madame Bovary was the only novel of Flaubert that Baudelaire discussed in print. Five years later, after the publication of *Salammbô* (1862), he incisively characterized the grandiose archaeological novel in a letter to his friend and publisher Poulet-Malassis: "What Flaubert has done, he alone was able to do. Entirely too much bric-a-brac, but many splendors, epic, historic, political, even animal. Something astonishing in the gesticulation of all the living beings" (*Corr.*, 2:271).

Baudelaire's flattering article on Théophile Gautier first appeared in *L'Artiste* on 13 March 1859; a month later it was issued in the form of a brochure. To the reader of today it seems somewhat disappointing not only because it lacks the provocative ideas that characterize so many of his essays, but also because it gives heroic stature to a writer who today is remembered less for his writing than for having introduced into literature the doctrine of art for art's sake.

Moreover, the amount of padding suggests that Baudelaire himself may have been somewhat lacking in inspiration. He includes two long direct passages from his essay *Notes nouvelles sur Edgar Poe*, a passage similar to one used in his essay *Les Drames et les romans honnêtes*, a long digression on the lack of artistic appreciation among the French people, and a penetrating, spontaneous eulogy of Balzac that contrasts with his more stilted praise of Gautier.

Moreover, the fact that Baudelaire admitted in his letter to Victor Hugo that he was aware of the lacunae in Gautier's astonishing mind and that, in his essay, he had sometimes "dissimulated rather than lied" indicates certain reservations on his part. True, he may also have been trying to win Hugo's favor and gain his consent to write a letter-preface for his brochure.

On the other hand, there are many reasons to believe that Baudelaire was sincere in his praise, for elsewhere in his entire correspondence he speaks of Gautier in the most flattering terms. What is even more indicative of his sincerity is that in a letter to his mother in 1857, Baudelaire expressed the certainty that his own work would some day take its place beside the best poems of Victor Hugo, Théophile Gautier, and Lord Byron. In his famous letter to Ancelle in 1866, he included the name of Gautier among those whom he considered the truly great of his time; equally important is the fact that Baudelaire chose Gautier as the subject of one of the five lectures he gave in Brussels.

Baudelaire's admiration for Gautier dated back to his youth and was shared by the poets of his generation, as Banville tells us in an unpublished poem. Fifteen years later, in the preface to *La Double vie (The Duality of Life)*, inspired and corrected by Baudelaire, Asselineau called Gautier "the most detached as well as the greatest of contemporary poets" (*OC*, 2:101). It was this preface that Crépet characterizes as "a veritable *Baudelairean manifesto*."[9]

If Baudelaire did feel certain reservations about Gautier's work, as may well have been the case, he obviously admired his disciplined art, his perfection of style and technique, and the harmony of his thought and word so deeply that, in his dedication of *Les Fleurs du mal* (1857) to the older poet, he could in all honesty describe him as "an impeccable poet, a perfect magician." In his essay of 1859 he remained dazzled by the "evocative magic" of Gautier's use of words.

Baudelaire found much to admire in Gautier in addition to his "evocative magic." Gautier's insistence on the autonomy of art, his belief that "as soon as a thing becomes useful, it ceases to be beautiful," his use of melancholy dominated by his obsession with death, and even, as in *Albertus,* his concern with moral evil, could only appeal to Baudelaire.

It is somewhat more difficult for the reader of today to see in Gautier, as the poet-critic maintained, a decipherer and translator of divine hieroglyphics who "showed an immense, innate understanding of universal *correspondences* and symbols" (*OC*, 2:117). In fairness to Gautier, however, it must be admitted that he was not entirely lacking in mystical qualities, since he himself maintained that "spirit is everything, matter exists only in appearance; the universe is perhaps only God's dream or an irradiation of the Word in the vastness of the cosmos."[10]

On the whole Baudelaire's analysis of Gautier is sound, although his criticism is generally less interesting than that found in many of his other essays. The reader of today finds much that is penetrating, though he cannot but feel that Baudelaire overestimated Gautier's short stories and art criticism and that he erred in maintaining that the poet's use of octosyllabic verse had all the majesty of the alexandrine. After all, Gautier himself had admitted in his *Histoire du romantisme* that the alexandrine was "too vast for these modest ambitions."

Judged as a whole, the critical ideas of Baudelaire, whether on art, music, or literature, are remarkably sound and acute. Though at one time he shared the neoclassical views of Banville and Louis Ménard, and at another the utilitarian concept of art espoused by Pierre Dupont and Proudhon, he soon found his own approach—one that "opened up the widest horizons" and allowed him to discover the admirable and eternal elements that constitute a work of art.

Although his debts to Diderot, Delacroix, and Poe, among others, are many, Baudelaire always succeeded in forging something new. Like his own fictional character Samuel Cramer, as I have already noted, he was "at the same time all the artists he had studied and all the books he had read, and yet, in spite of this talent for mimicry, he remained profoundly original" (*OC,* 1:554).

Chapter Four
Les Fleurs du mal

Baudelaire's chief claim to fame is his volume of verse, *Les Fleurs du mal,* in which is to be found a strange amalgam of old and new. Classic in its clarity, discipline, and reliance on traditional forms, romantic in its subjectivity, its spirit of revolt, and its macabre elements, *Les Fleurs du mal* is also considered a forerunner of Surrealism in its use of dreams, myths, and fantasies. Far more important, however, is the fact that by its use of suggestion, it anticipates Symbolism and opens the door to modern poetry.

Among Baudelaire's most important innovations is his use of correspondences. Although in his essays he refers to the transcendental correspondences between the visible and the invisible worlds, it is the synesthetic correspondences between colors, sounds, and perfumes that he employs in both his poetry and prose.

Even more characteristic is his use of the correspondences between exterior nature and his own inner world. By finding symbols in outer reality that correspond to and suggest his inner thoughts and feelings, he often succeeds in creating what he himself called "a suggestive magic . . . containing the world exterior to the artist and the artist himself"—a suggestive magic leaving a "lacuna," as he wrote in his essay on Wagner, "to be filled by the reader" (*OC,* 2:598, 782). Such use of the symbol not only allowed him to exteriorize his idea or mood by giving concrete form to the abstract, but also helped him achieve what he termed an "indispensable obscurity" that stopped short of being hermetic.

Baudelaire introduced a number of stylistic innovations that have since been adopted by most modern poets. As a result of his emphasis on suggestion, the image, no longer peripheral, often becomes the very essence of the poem. His tendency to introduce a prosaic or even crude image in the midst of an otherwise highly poetic style, as well as his remarkable ability to treat sordid reality without losing poetic elevation, has been widely imitated. Equally characteristic are his musical sonorities, his subtle and suggestive rhythms, his frequent use of monologue or dialogue to achieve dramatic effect, and his mingling of the grand manner with a quiet, subdued, and conversational tone.

The unifying theme running throughout the six sections of *Les Fleurs du mal* is that of the conflict between good and evil, spleen and ideal, dream and reality. Obsessed with a belief in original sin and in the duality of man, and using his own personal experience as raw material, Baudelaire examines the spiritual problems of his age with probing, almost brutal self-analysis.

That the unity of *Les Fleurs du mal* springs from Baudelaire's personal experience is attested by his letter to Ancelle, written from Brussels on 18 February 1866: "Must I tell you, you who have not guessed it more than the others, that in this *atrocious* book, I have put all my *heart,* all my *love,* all my *religion* (travestied), all my hate? It is true that I shall write the contrary, that I shall swear by all the gods that it is a book of *pure art,* of *mimicry,* of virtuosity, and I shall be a shameless liar" (*Corr., 2:610*).

It should be noted, however, that it was only as a sort of afterthought that Baudelaire, like Balzac, came to view his work as a sort of unified whole, although he had obviously been conscious of its vague unity even in 1857. It was in an effort to emphasize this unity that he not only changed the order of the sections in the 1861 edition, but also added an additional section entitled "Tableaux parisiens." At the same time, he increased the total number of poems to 126, after removing the six that had been banned by the court.

Inspired by Barbey d'Aurevilly's 1857 comment regarding the "secret architecture" of *Les Fleurs du mal,* critics have often adopted the same term. Barbey's remark may also have encouraged the poet to stress the unity of the 1861 edition to Alfred de Vigny to whom he wrote: "All the new poems have been made to be adapted to an unusual framework which I have chosen" (*Corr., 2:196*). In each section, however, there are poems that seem to have little or nothing to do with the plan of the ensemble—further proof that the so-called architecture was only an afterthought.

"Au lecteur"

The introductory poem, "Au lecteur" ("To the Reader"), serves as a sort of preface to the entire volume and has for its theme the conflict between good and evil—a conflict that besets all mankind and in which evil remains triumphant. We are reminded of a notation made by Baudelaire in his *Journaux intimes:* "There is in every man at all times two simultaneous impulses—the one toward God, the other toward Satan" (*OC,* 1:682). In "Au Lecteur" Baudelaire stresses the postulation toward Satan ("It is the Devil who pulls the strings") that manifests itself in all humanity—in the poet as well as in the reader who, in the last line, is addressed dramatically and ironically as "hypocrite lecteur, mon frère, mon semblable." Thus the poem becomes, as Claude Pichois has so aptly stated, a *tu quoque* rather than a *mea culpa* (*OC,* 1:831).

Of all the sins that beset us, none is greater than *ennui* which Baudelaire sees not as the "taedium vitae" of the ancients nor as the *mal du siècle* of the Romantics. For him, it is rather a spiritual illness, a paralysis of the mind or a lethargy that, by preventing us from realizing our ideal, allows evil to be victorious in its conflict with the good.

In style, the poem is a strange mixture of sixteenth-century eloquence and rhetoric, entirely consistent with its sermonizing character, and of the realistic, crude images often called "shock images": "beggars nourishing their vermin"; "shadows that stink"; "kissing and biting the breast of a whore." This blend of stylistic effects will be seen to characterize many of the poems that appear throughout the volume and will be widely imitated in much of the poetry that is to follow that of Baudelaire.

Spleen et idéal

The first cycle of poems, entitled *Spleen et idéal,* begins, despite the word order of the title, with poems that pertain more or less closely to the category of the *Idéal.* In fact, the first twenty-one poems are all related to the problems facing the artist and to the nature of beauty. Jacques Crépet and Georges Blin subdivide the cycle of *Idéal* into two subcycles: one on art, and one on love. The cycle of art is further divided into three parts dealing with the grandeur of the poet, the misery of the poet, and the poet's concept of beauty.

The opening poem, "Bénédiction," with its autobiographical allusions, utilizes two themes dear to the Romanticists: that of the misunderstood poet, mocked and persecuted by society, despised and cursed by wife and mother; and that of the poet's redemption through suffering and through his knowledge that, after death, he will find a place reserved for him among the ranks of the blessed. Despite a style that, in general, is overly forced and rhetorical, the poet achieves in the last lines a simple, almost incantory beauty.

"L'Albatros," a poem much admired by Flaubert, treats, like its companion piece "Bénédiction" but far more effectively, the romantic theme of the isolation of the poet. Though it did not appear in the 1857 edition of *Les Fleurs du mal,* it may well have been composed around the time of his voyage of 1841–42 and published at a later date. The addition of the third strophe at the suggestion of Asselineau evidently satisfied any reservations the poet may have had about its readiness for publication. Like Vigny's

"Moïse," the poem is symbolic in the traditional manner. But whereas
Moses is a majestic, powerful figure, solitary but deeply respected and
feared, the albatross, the "prince of clouds" and "king of azure skies," is superb in flight but comic and clumsy on earth, prevented from walking by
his giant wings. The poem is thus built on a traditional antithesis: the contrast between the genius of the poet (his grandeur) and his inability to adapt
himself to an indifferent and hostile society (his misery). Here as in later
poems, Baudelaire reveals his belief in the duality of man; but whereas he is
usually concerned with the duality resulting from the conflict between good
and evil, in "L'Albatros" he is symbolizing the conflict between the artist's
genius and uncomprehending and hostile society.

Following "L'Albatros" is one of Baudelaire's loveliest poems, "Elévation." Marked by a joyous, rhapsodic emotion, a spiritual and physical ecstasy, an intimate understanding of mute things, and a soaring rhythm that
suggests the beating wings of a bird in flight, the poem has been interpreted
in different ways by critics seeking to determine the nature of the poetic experience. That the experience is one provoked by listening to music seems
the most plausible, given Baudelaire's reaction elsewhere in his work to
what he calls the "lyric manner," described by him in his essay on Banville:
"the soul is, as it were, illuminated by it . . . carried away; our whole being
rises in the air . . . as if to a higher region" (*OC,* 2:164).

The striking similarity between Baudelaire's description of this "lyric
manner of feeling" and his choice of imagery in "Elévation" is even more apparent in his essay on Wagner in which the poet's evocation of the German
composer's overture to *Lohengrin* seems at times a paraphrase of the poem
written many years earlier.[1] In both poem and essay, the abstract subject is
defined in physical terms that are strikingly similar.

It is true that Baudelaire's feeling of soaring in space, his idea of the ascent of the spirit into the luminous confines of the starry spheres, is also
fairly common in the literature of the Romantics. Overlooked is the fact that
the most important of these Romantic influences was the *Kreisleriana* of
E. T. A. Hoffmann, greatly admired by Baudelaire, in which certain passages describing music seem to suggest the very genesis of the poem. So frequent are the allusions in the *Kreisleriana* to an ascent into space, to the
"soul that takes its flight above earthly sufferings" that the poet, given his
enthusiasm for "the divine Hoffmann," appears not to have escaped his con-
tagious influence.[2] Nor should it be forgotten that the prose poem "Le
Thyrse," dedicated to Franz Liszt, begins with the same rhythm as
"Elévation." Apparently the mere remembrance of a particular type of

music was capable of re-creating in the poet's mind the ecstatic vision to which he has given expression.

It is in "Les Correspondances" that Baudelaire, as we have seen, voices his conception of correspondences—a doctrine that was not new, as he was fully aware—in a poem that was to be adopted by the Symbolists as a manifesto. In the first quatrain, the poet evokes what is sometimes called "vertical" correspondences—those that exist between the visible and invisible forms of the universe. In other words, the visible forms of the world here below are only symbols of an invisible, higher reality, or what Plato calls "images of a divine copy."

In the second quatrain, the poet evokes the horizontal correspondences that exist between the things of this world—perfumes, colors, and sounds —which have not only the power to suggest each other but also to suggest feelings, moods, or ideas. It was largely through the use of horizontal correspondences that Baudelaire succeeded in revolutionizing poetic expression and in creating what he himself once called "a suggestive magic." The poem itself, as Lloyd James Austin suggests, is a practical application of the doctrine the poet presents.[3] To affirm the fundamental harmony and unity of all sensations, Baudelaire employs visual, auditory, olfactory, tactile, and kinesthetic images, all presented with a grandeur of style that results from the poem's dignity and clarity and from what Crépet has called its "gnomic splendor."

In contrast to the ecstasy that marks "Elévation" and "Correspondances," the poem beginning "J'aime le souvenir" reveals the poet's temptation to forget the ugliness of the modern world and to find his inspiration in the beauty of the past. Despite this inclination, however, and consistent with his desire to "turn mud into gold," he determines to seek inspiration in the ugliness that surrounds him.

"Les Phares" ("Beacons") evokes the oeuvre of eight artists by summarizing, within four lines assigned to each one, the general atmosphere that pervades their work. Baudelaire himself has commented on the verse devoted to Delacroix: "Lake of blood"—red; "haunted by evil angels"—surnaturalism; "a wood always green"—green, the complementary color of red; "a gloomy sky"—the tumultuous and stormy depths of his paintings; "fanfares from Weber"—ideas of romantic music that awaken the harmony of his color (*OC,* 2:595). In the last three verses, in which ecstasies and the *Te Deum* mingle with cries, tears, and blasphemies, the themes of all the artists are summarized, as it were. Given form in art, they serve as proof of mankind's dignity.

The following five poems reveal the various difficulties faced by the poet.

"La Muse malade," an early poem, expresses ideas characteristic of the Pagan School, which Baudelaire soon came to renounce after encountering the influence of Delacroix. In it, the poet compares the "madness and horror" of present-day poetry with the robust poetry of the distant past and recognizes in the modern muse one that had become "ill" and degenerate. In "La Muse vénale" he laments the necessity of the modern poet to prostitute his art in order to win the approval of the common herd. In "Le Mauvais Moine" ("The Bad Monk"), the poet accuses himself of his idleness and his failure to transform his misery into a thing of beauty, much as monks had once done in embellishing the mighty walls of old cloisters with paintings of the images of death. As a result of his neglect, Baudelaire's soul has become a tomb whose walls remain eternally unadorned like those of some "odious cloister."

In what is by far the loveliest of the five poems, "L'Ennemi," Baudelaire, comparing the poet's soul to a garden devastated by a storm, expresses his fear that the new flowers of which he dreams may fail to find sufficient nourishment. The identity of the enemy that gnaws at the poet's heart has been subject to various explanations. Critics have suggested Time, Ennui, Death, Remorse, Satan—all of which could well explain his inability to achieve his goal. It is possible, however, that the poet may have been thinking either of his tendency to procrastinate—a fault of which he often complained—or of his fear of losing his poetic faculties. Six months later he will confide to his mother this very fear (*OC*, 1:327).

"Guignon" ("Ill Luck"), which follows "L'Ennemi," expresses an idea Baudelaire had ridiculed as a youth but later came to accept as an explanation of his own destiny as well as that of Edgar Allan Poe. The poem is an amalgam of Thomas Grey's "Elegy in a Country Churchyard" and Longfellow's "A Psalm of Life." Very well known in France, Grey's "Elegy" had been translated by several writers, including Chateaubriand. Baudelaire had been haunted by the poem and had actually used a passage from it as an epigram for his poem "Les Plaintes d'un Icare" ("The Complaint of Icarus"). He had also imitated Grey in his poem "Les Hiboux" ("Owls").

The three poems following "L'Ennemi" suggest, as Alison Fairlie has remarked, a "fusion of longing and loveliness, restlessness and mystery."[4] The finest of the three is undoubtedly "La Vie antérieure" ("A Former Life"), which has for its theme the sensuous pleasure aroused by the exotic beauty of the scene that is evoked. Though critics have vied with each other in suggesting the sources for the poem, it is undeniable that one of those sources must have been memories brought back from the sea voyage made in his youth. The dreamlike atmosphere, with its rich, majestic, and solemn beauty, is made more mysterious by its reference to the "secret douleureux" that troubles and saddens the poet. It is interesting, moreover, to note that in *L'Exposition de 1855* Baudelaire also refers to the "secret douleureux" he finds hidden in the eyes of the women painted by Delacroix.

"Bohémiens en Voyage" ("Gypsies on the Road"), inspired by the prints of Jacques Callot, describes the trek of a group of ragged but proud gypsies in search of a better life. As depicted by the poet, they seem to symbolize the artist or poet who longingly seeks in the future the recognition that constantly eludes him. In "L'Homme et la mer" ("Man and the Sea"), the poet recognizes the sea as a mirror in which he finds his own image. Implacable brothers, both contain within their fathomless depths unknown riches kept secret from the world around them.

"Don Juan aux enfers" ("Don Juan in Hell") and "Châtiment de l'orgueil" ("The Punishment of Pride") both concern pride devoid of all that is human. Inspired by the canvases of Delacroix, the poet depicts a proud Don Juan, incapable of love, pity, and remorse, who is beyond all good and evil. "Châtiments de l'orgueil," based on sources that go back to the Middle Ages, reveals the self-destruction that results from man's desire to rival the power of the Creator.

Although "La Beauté" has been subjected to various interpretations, there seems little doubt that in it Baudelaire is describing a beauty divorced from earthly passion. It has often been pointed out that his use of the expression "clartés éternelles," seen in the sightless eyes of the sculpted goddess, is reminiscent of Poe's exclamation in *Ligeia:* "Those eyes! those shining, those divine orbs!"

Even more noteworthy is the fact that under the influence of Poe, Baudelaire had modified his own theory of the relationship of passion to poetry and had temporarily adopted the American poet's belief that "passion is *natural,* too natural not to introduce an offensive discordant note into the domain of pure beauty" (*OC,* 2:334). Of all forms of beauty, it is the cold, unresponsive goddess that for him best symbolizes the unattainable and passionless beauty for which artist and poet yearn in vain.

Le Salon de 1859 contains ideas that are strikingly similar: "What a glance in those pupilless eyes! Just as lyric poetry makes everything noble— even passion; so sculpture, true sculpture, makes everything solemn—even movement; it bestows upon everything that is human something eternal. . . ." (*OC,* 2:671). The reader is reminded of the last lines of the poem: "For to fascinate these docile lovers, I have . . . my eyes, my large eyes with their eternal light!"

"L'Idéal" and "La Géante" reveal the poet's taste for the bizarre and the monumental. "The beautiful is always strange," he had written in 1855, and in *Le Salon de 1859* he confessed his preference, other things being equal, for the large both in nature and in art (*OC*, 2:578, 646). In the two concluding poems of *Spleen,* entitled "Le Masque" and "Hymne à la Beauté," Baudelaire reverts to a more tragic conception of life. Based on the statuette *La Comédie humaine,* sculpted by Ernest Christophe and exhibited in the Salon of 1859, "Le Masque" portrays a woman smiling provocatively. Seen from either side, however, her face is discovered to be a mask hiding features contorted by pain and grief. What had first delighted our eyes, Baudelaire explains, is the universal mask beneath which is hidden our secret griefs and suffering. And the poet concludes with lines that express his own weariness and despair: "Tomorrow, alas, she must live again like us / Tomorrow, the next day, and for eternity."

Baudelaire's question in "Hymne à la Beauté" pertaining to the origin of beauty has in it nothing scandalous or perverse.[5] Written in the last tragic years of his life, it is not the product of a taste for frenetic Romanticism, but rather of the philosophical and aesthetic beliefs that mark his works of that period.

The poem derives first of all from his conviction that art, of which beauty is the goal, is the result of the duality of man, who is "simultaneously impelled by good and evil"; and second, from his belief that evil, when purified by art, can be transmuted into beauty. Intermingled with these two themes is a third: the effect of beauty on those who perceive it. Just as beauty has its origin in man's dual nature, so the effects of beauty are likewise determined by that dual nature. Thus beauty may produce either "benevolence or crime," "joy or disaster."

For the poet, however, beauty's chief value lies in its power to satisfy his longing for the infinite. Appearing for the first time in the penultimate stanza and interrupting the antithetical structure of the poem, the principal theme—"if you [beauty] open the door of an infinite that I love and have never seen"—is made all the more moving and climactic by its Racinian simplicity. For the desperately unhappy poet, beauty, despite all, is to be worshipped, since by making time less heavy and the universe less hideous, it serves as a means of escaping the human condition.

The Love Poetry

The love poems that follow "A la Beauté" are divided into three main groups, each devoted to one of the three women with whom he was emotionally involved.

The Black Venus: Jeanne Duval The poems celebrating Jeanne Duval evoke the physical passion and despair aroused by the exotic beauty of a woman incapable of appreciating either his genius or his love. It was for her that the poet wrote "Les Bijoux" ("Jewels"), which opened the cycle of love poems in the 1857 edition of *Les Fleurs du mal*. One of the six to be banned by the court, it was later to be included in *Les Epaves*.

"Les Bijoux" is almost as much a reflection of Baudelaire's temperament as it is of his mistress' charm and beauty. Though concerned with the physical aspect of love, the expression of the poet's eroticism, far from being lewd, has some of the magnificence of the Song of Songs. Its sensuality, cerebral and aesthetic, reminds us of Samuel Cramer, who loved the human body as a piece of perfect architecture inspired with movement. Although based on personal memories, they are seen through the images and style of Delacroix—particularly those of his odalisques—and are largely responsible for emphasizing the aesthetic, as opposed to the erotic, character of the poem.

The treatment of the theme is mainly plastic, with only two images of sound—the tinkling of the bracelets and the crackling of the fire—interrupting the visual images. The last verse leaves the reader with a sense of quiet repose as the flickering lamp dies down and the room remains in darkness, with only the firelight casting its reflections on the woman's tawny skin.

"Parfum exotique" and "La Chevelure" ("Her Hair") are both inspired by the perfume of Jeanne's hair and breast which, by awakening in the poet the exotic beauty of tropical lands and of a blue-black sea, offer him an escape from the bleak ugliness of the present. Memory thus becomes both the theme and the method, but unlike the involuntary memory of Proust, that of Baudelaire is a matter of deliberate recall.[6] Both poems are also examples of his use of correspondences, of perfumes suggesting both sounds and sights—the sight of a port, filled with sails and masts, and the sound of songs, sung by sailors, echoing in the air. Unlike "L'Albatros," which presents an idea, both poems depict a state of mind through a series of images whose sole purpose is to create a unity of sentiments and emotions. The rich music, the variety of rhythms, and the majesty of the lines make "La Chevelure," in particular, one of Baudelaire's finest poems.

After the ecstasy expressed in his earlier poems, in those pertaining to spleen Baudelaire depicts the torment and degradation of a passion that remains unreciprocated. His verse now reveals a mingling of love and hate, a loathing not only of his own weakness and debasement but even more of

Jeanne, whom he now views as a "cruel and implacable animal," and as "the queen of sins." The love-hate relationship is especially evident in the untitled poem beginning "Je t'adore à l'égal de la voûte nocturne" in which, incidentally, the use of the poetic "clair obscur" (is he speaking of the moon or a woman?) does much to explain its fascination. The contrast between the sublimity of the first part of the poem with the macabre and repugnant lines that follow produces a feeling of shock and surprise that lend proof to Auerbach's claim that Baudelaire "gave this age a new poetic style; a mixture of the base and contemptible with the sublime, a symbolic use of realistic horror which was unprecedented in lyric poetry."[7]

Nowhere is this "mixture of the base and contemptible with the sublime" more evident than in his poem "Une Charogne" ("Carrion"), written before the end of 1843. And perhaps nowhere has he given better proof of his contention that "the horrible, artistically expressed, becomes beauty" (OC, 2:123). Though its theme, based on the conquest of time and death by great art, is borrowed from the Renaissance, its treatment is strictly Baudelairean. Choosing, no doubt deliberately, the rhythm used in Lamartine's "Le Lac," the poet employs images that insist on ugliness and horror. Moreover, his exaggerated courtesy and ceremonious manner in addressing his beloved with the formal *vous* rather than the familiar *tu* further increase the ironical effect, as does the poet's reminder that, through his verse, he will preserve the "divine essence" of their love, despite the vermin that will destroy her once beautiful body.

The poems that follow "Une Charogne" further illustrate the love-hate relationship that existed between the poet and Jeanne. Baudelaire sees himself as the victim of a vampire ("Le Vampire") from whom escape is impossible, more because of his own abject desire to remain than because of the power of his tormentor. The cold, cruel eyes of Jeanne are like those of a cat ("Le Chat") that seem as if made of metal. In what appears to be Hell itself, the lovers struggle to the very death ("Duellum"). And in "De Profundis clamavi" the poet longs jealously for the stupid sleep of lowly animals—a sleep in which the torments of life are finally obliterated.

The frenzied hate expressed in "Duellum" is in striking contrast to the tender love that marks "Le Balcon." One of Baudelaire's loveliest poems, it belongs to the second crisis (1856) of his liaison with Jeanne. The feelings of nostalgia, regret, and deep sadness that he expressed in a letter to his mother on 11 September 1856, in which he recounts his loneliness and sorrow, are clearly reflected in the poem. That it was written before his reconciliation with Jeanne seems entirely plausible, given the poet's use of the past tense and the absense of the love-hate relationship that existed during their years spent together, as well as the very words with which he begins the poem: "Mère des souvenirs."

Containing neither narration nor argument, the entire poem is simply an evocation of a state of mind, of past happiness, and of love relived in memory and translated through harmony of sound and a slow, dreamlike rhythm. By the use of refrains that enclose each stanza, he succeeds not only in giving the poem a certain unity but also in adding to the musical effect of the whole. In the last line of the poem, the slight but subtle change in the wording of the refrain (a simple change from "those" to "oh!") adds to the poet's revery a note of finality and of longing and brings to an end his dream of past happiness.

The cycle of Jeanne ends with two poems in which Baudelaire bids farewell to all that the black Venus had represented in his life: beauty, sadness, ecstasy, bitterness, and hate. The sonnet sequence entitled "Un Fantôme" is an attempt on his part to find, in Proustian fashion, "dans le présent le passé restauré" ("the past restored to the present"). In spite of debilitating illness that had destroyed her beauty, the poet defies Time, "black assassin of Life and Art" ever to destroy the memory of one who had been his "joy and his glory." In "Je te donne ces vers" ("I give you these verses"), Baudelaire recalls once again Jeanne's beauty and coldness and in lines that are classic in their beauty and dignity, promises that his verses—a "vessel favored by a strong north wind"—will carry her memory into the distant future.

The Blonde Venus: Mme Sabatier   The cycle of poems belonging to Mme Sabatier, known as the blonde Venus, parallels the same sequence of experiences found in the cycle devoted to Jeanne. In the early poems inspired by the black Venus, Baudelaire had begun by celebrating her animal grace and exotic beauty. Only later did he voice the contradictory and powerful emotions resulting from their love-hate relationship.

In the case of Mme Sabatier, the poet likewise begins by singing praises of her charm, her gaiety, and what he regards as her spiritual qualities. In the 1861 edition of *Les Fleurs du mal,* the cycle begins with the Latin title "Semper Eadem," a poem of transition in which the bittersweet memories of Jeanne still haunt the poet. Knowing love to be but a "lie," he nevertheless attempts to seek the understanding and solace of one who, in later poems, he will address as his "guardian angel, his Muse, and his Madonna."

As in the cycle of the black Venus, the poems that immediately follow are filled with ecstasy, but with an ecstasy that is usually lacking in sensuality and expressed in terms of religious adoration. In the case of Jeanne, the poet had been intoxicated by her animal grace and her exotic beauty; in Mme Sabatier, it is her eyes shining with a "mystic light" that fascinate and lead him in the "path of Beauty" ("Le Flambeau vivant"). The blonde Venus is for him both Muse and Madonna; in "Réversibilité" she is an "ange de gaieté . . . de bonté . . . de santé . . . de beauté . . . de bonheur." And in the closing lines of the poem he asks pointedly and with deliberate intent *not* for her love, but for her prayers.

Soon, however, as he had done in the cycle of Jeanne, Baudelaire introduces sentiments marked by a note of bitterness and disillusionment. In "A Celle qui est trop gaie" ("To One Who Is Too Gay"), now found in *Les Epaves,* the poet, after picturing Madame Sabatier's gaiety, her charming smile, and her dress of variegated colors resembling a ballet of flowers, suddenly admits a feeling of both hate and love and expresses a desire to destroy her joy and health that contrasts so strongly with his own bitterness and perversity. In "Confessions," it is Mme Sabatier herself who plaintively confides to the poet the harsh realities of the life hidden beneath her mask of gaiety and laughter.

"Harmonie du Soir," like "Le Balcon," evokes a feeling of peace and nostalgia that is explained only in the last line of the poem where the poet refers to the memory of a loved one that "shines within him like a monstrance." Devoid of any "intellectual armature" or of any suggestion of physical love, the entire poem is simply the expression of a state of mind—a feeling of nostalgia, melancholy, and repose. No better example can be found of Baudelaire's definition of pure poetry as "a suggestive magic . . . containing the world exterior to the artist and the artist himself" (*OC,* 2:598).

Unlike the ornamental or explanatory imagery of the Romantics, that of "Harmonie du Soir" is purely suggestive and deliberately obscure. Either secular or drawn from the Catholic liturgy, the images are themselves the poem. Their obscurity concurs with Baudelaire's belief, expressed in his essay on Wagner, that "In music, as in painting, and even in the written word . . . there is always a lacuna completed by the imagination of the listener" (*OC,* 2:781–82). In his *Journaux intimes,* there is likewise a notation that perfectly characterizes the beauty of the poem: "Beauty is something ardent and sad, something a little vague, leaving room for conjecture" (*OC,* 1:657).

The emotions produced by the imagery are further enhanced by the use of a rhythm that suggests the slow movement of a languorous waltz, by the choice of words that evoke the sensuous harmony of music, and by the use of repetition, which aids in the creation of an incantatory effect. Sound and meaning have become inseparable, and "Harmonie du Soir" remains one of Baudelaire's most musical of poems.

The cycle of Mme Sabatier ends with the poem "Le Flacon" ("The Flask"), which plays the same role as does "Je te donne ces vers" in the cycle of Jeanne. Long after the poet is dead and forgotten, the verses in which he had perpetuated the memory of the blond Venus will be like the fragrance of a perfume that lingers in an old dusty bottle found many years later in the depths of some dark closet.

The Blonde Venus: Marie Daubrun   The cycle of Marie Daubrun, beginning with "Le Poison," is inspired neither by the tormented passion he had felt for Jeanne nor by the more idealistic love expressed in his poems to Mme Sabatier. Instead, these verses voice the ambivalent emotions of one who has known disillusionment and despair and whose poems reflect the anguish of desire and the fear of inevitable deception.

Baudelaire associates the beauty of the green-eyed actress with autumn's misty skies and threatening clouds, dispelled at times by sudden bursts of sunshine. In her eyes he sees reflected both tenderness and cruelty, and he remains haunted by the thought of the coming of "implacable winter" (old age) with its sharp and icy pleasures. In "Le Beau Navire" ("The Beautiful Ship") the graceful, swaying movement of Marie's walk is compared to that of a beautiful vessel moving with a slow, gentle rhythm on the open sea. But it is especially the eyes of the actress that so often attract and fascinate the poet. Like "shining beacon lights," they reflect in their mysterious depths now laughter, now tears. And, like the intent eyes of a beautiful cat (celebrated in a second poem by that title), their magnetic power seems to catch and hold the glance of the poet.

One of the loveliest poems Baudelaire wrote for Marie, "L'Invitation au voyage," is a perfect example of the "pure art" he had described in "L'Art philosophique": "a suggestive magic containing both . . . the world exterior to the artist and the artist himself" (*OC,* 2:598). Its tone of intimacy coupled with solemnity, its melodic fluidity, its verbal magic, and its use of the refrain all give it a songlike quality that has caused it to be often set to music. Once again Baudelaire has effected a return to "the lost Eden,"—an imaginary Holland that lives only in his dreams, a paradise which he hopes to share with his beloved and which he creates with the power of his imagination.

The fact that the poet addresses Marie as "sister" may be an indication of love devoid of sensuality. More likely, however, Baudelaire was thinking of the Song of Songs in which the word *sister* is used to designate the beloved.

As in other poems written for Marie, the images are those of misty skies, autumn sun, and cloudy days. In the first stanza, Marie is invited to go with the poet to a country whose beauty resembles her own. In the following stanza, he evokes the richness, the tranquillity, the ornate splendor of the home they would share. In the third stanza, the dream has become a reality and, addressing Marie as if they were already there, he invites her to admire with him the drowsy ships, the fields of hay, the canals, and the city "colored in hyacinth and gold."

The extraordinary musical effect resulting from the poem's rhythm and harmony is further enhanced by a refrain that summarizes in five abstract nouns (luxe, calme, volupté, ordre, et beauté) both the beauty of the objects evoked as well as the effect they have produced on the poet himself. In addition to the suggestive magic that Baudelaire has so successfully created, the poem perfectly demonstrates his belief that rhythm is the most useful of instruments in the creation of beauty.

One of the most beautiful poems in the French language, "Chant d'automne," written for Marie in 1859, has for its theme the pitiless march of time and the poet's desire to sweeten a destiny from which there is no escape. An example of those correspondences that link the exterior world to the inner world of the artist (the winter of life and the winter of indifferent nature), it is also proof of Baudelaire's belief that "in certain, almost 'surnaturel' states of mind, the whole of life is revealed in the spectacle, ordinary as it may be, that appears before our eyes. It becomes its very symbol" (*OC,* 1:659).

The point of departure is indeed one of the most commonplace events of life: the thud of falling logs being stored in the courtyard in preparation for the coming of winter—a winter that, the poet admits, has turned his heart into a block of ice. In the following verses, the poet employs a series of auditory images drawn from the outside world that, echoing the sound of the falling wood, reveal his despondent state of mind: the blows of a battering-ram against a tower and the sound of a coffin being nailed in haste.

The second part of the poem, in which the poet speaks quietly and tenderly to Marie, seems at first glance completely unrelated to the preceding. The reader soon discovers, however, that Baudelaire sees himself in the autumn of life and that he is regretting the "white and torrid summer" that has gone forever. As for Marie, her beauty and gentleness are to him like the soft, golden rays of autumn's end that has come to replace a passion, dead though not forgotten.

In "L'Irréparable," a sense of ecstasy is replaced by a sense of disquiet. Suffering from a feeling of inescapable torment and from the memory of a past that can never be erased, Baudelaire longs in vain for the traditional fairy who, at the end of a pantomine in which Marie had once taken part, comes to destroy the forces of evil. "Causerie" ("Conversation") continues on the same note of hopelessness and despair. Love and heartbreak are replaced by a feeling of gentle melancholy, and Marie's love, like a "beautiful autumn sky," fails to halt the sadness that "mounts within [him] like the sea," leaving only the "burning memory of its bitter mire."

The cycle of Marie ends with a baroque poem, "A une Madone," which contains a strange mixture of love, hate, jealousy, and revenge. The subtitle "Ex-Voto dans le goût espagnol" seems an attempt to explain the mingling of religious and erotic elements as well as the savage emotions unleased by the poet. As in the case of Jeanne, Baudelaire will preserve the memory of the torment and beauty of their former love by symbolically constructing an altar for her. But unlike the tribute of love he promised to pay the memory of Jeanne, he thinks only of revenge and threatens to plant in Marie's "panting, bleeding heart" seven knives fashioned from the seven deadly sins. The rich, ornate style employed throughout the entire poem adds a note of aesthetic dignity that contrasts sharply with the sadistic violence to which the poet gives vent.

In other poems, "Les Chats," "Les Hiboux" ("Owls"), "La Pipe," and "La Musique," the poet adopts a lighter tone before yielding to the somber mood that characterizes the actual spleen poems themselves as well as the two that immediately precede, "Le Mort joyeux" and "Le Tonneau de la Haine" ("The Cask of Hate"). In "Le Mort joyeux" the better known of the two, critics have accused Baudelaire of sadism, of a desire to shock the public, and of an attempt to emulate Edgar Allan Poe. Antoine Adam, on the other hand, wisely refuses to take the poem seriously and views it as a pose much like that affected by the young Romantics known as "bousingos."[8]

There is also a strong possibility that the poem is the result of the poet's use of irony and of a belief, as he states in *Fusées,* that "irony and surnaturalism" are "two fundamental literary qualities" (*OC,* 1:658). The morbidity of Poe may indeed be here, but certainly not the American poet's fascination and sensual taste for death and the dead. To prefer to have his decomposed body eaten by worms and crows rather than "to implore a tear" from the public is rather the reaction of one who, in his exasperation, attempts to convince his readers that the destruction of the body by worms and crows is nothing compared to the cruelty of life.

It is only with "La Cloche fêlée" ("The Cracked Bell"), which was entitled "Spleen" in 1851, that Baudelaire, attempting to escape his spleen, yields to his anguish and accepts its inevitability. For him, as he wrote his mother on

30 December 1857, spleen is really "a sort of metaphysical malady, a complete paralysis of the mind and the emotions, a feeling of discouragement and unbelievable isolation, a total lack of desires" (*Corr.*, 1:438). The poem is a magnificent example of that "suggestive magic" in which the poet suggests his state of mind—the fear of having lost his poetic genius—by evoking correspondences in the exterior world.

The entire structure of the poem depends on a central comparison between the poet's soul and a flawed bell and on a secondary comparison between the flawed genius of the poet and a wounded soldier lying on the edge of a lake of blood, vainly struggling beneath a mound of dead. For Baudelaire, the futile struggle of the dying soldier is a reminder of his own desperate attempts to express his poetic genius and thus "to people the cold air of the night with his songs."

In "Pluviose," another example of "pure poetry," Baudelaire evokes the physical ambience that provokes his spleen. In the first quatrain, the cold, the rain, the fog, and the cemetery, seen from his window, all suggest death and decay. In the following verses, the room itself—the smoking log, the uncarpeted floor, the thin, mangy cat, the wheezing clock—only reinforce the impression of gloom. Nowhere does the poet better reveal his ability to extract beauty from ugliness and to mingle the grand style, found in the opening quatrain, with the prosaic realism of what follows. Here also Baudelaire reveals a suggestive power that borders on the vague and mysterious and that brings alive every object within and without the room, from the wheezing clock, the hissing log, and the tolling of the bell to the sound of the rain in the gutters of the roof that reminds him of the soul of some wandering old poet.

And finally, turning from the descriptive to the hallucinatory, the poet notes a pack of old cards left by a "dropsical old woman" in which the Jack of Hearts and the Queen of Spades seem to be talking "sinisterly" of their dead loves. Once again, Baudelaire reveals his extraordinary ability to endow ugliness and poverty with the "suggestive magic" that for him characterized pure poetry.

Best known and the most powerful of the Spleen poems is one beginning "Quand le ciel bas et lourd" ("When the low heavy sky"), in which the poet exteriorizes his state of mind and symbolizes his fear, his anguish, and his despair by the use of a series of sinister and completely unrelated images. The poem consists of but two sentences the first of which includes all but the last stanza. In the first three verses, Baudelaire employs striking visual images that evoke a feeling of oppression: the low, heavy sky that weighs like a lid on the poet's spirit; the dank cell in which a timid bat strikes its head against the rotting masonry; the rain that, streaking the windowpanes, suggests the bars of a prison; and finally the loathsome spiders that seem to spin their webs in the poet's very brain.

The silence of the first three stanzas, each beginning with "when," is suddenly broken in the fourth. Visual images are replaced by the auditory: the wild, loud clamor of bells reverberating in the poet's head, and the unceasing groans of wandering, homeless spirits. Hope, vanquished, weeps, and "atrocious" Anguish hoists its black banner over the poet's bowed head. The cumulative effect of the images and the final crescendo, broken in the penultimate line by the choked sobs of Hope, produce on the reader an almost shattering effect that is further enhanced by the slow, heavy rhythm and the use of the grand style which, strangely enough, adds a note of sublimity to images that are completely incompatible with the sublime.

The poems that follow are among the most nihilistic ever written by Baudelaire. Nature itself reflects his fear and abhorrence of life. The great woods, like great cathedrals, echo to the sound of the *De profundis* and the poet longs for the stark blackness of a starless night in "Obsession"; time is swallowing him up much as the snow envelopes a body grown stiff from the cold in "Le Goût du néant" ("The Thirst for Nothingness"); the clouds seem to form a shroud in which he discovers the presence of a loved one ("Alchimie de la douleur"); and in the blackness of the clouds he sees not only the hearses of his dreams but also the reflection of the "Hell in which [his] heart delights" ("Horreur sympathique").

It is especially in these Spleen poems that Baudelaire, like Racine, shows himself the master of the single line whose beauty and poignancy is almost impossible to translate: "I am like a cemetery abhorred by the moon"; "Avalanche, will you carry me away in your fall"; "the adorable springtime has lost its perfume."

One of the most sadistic and masochistic of his poems, "L'Héautontimoroumenos" ("The Self-Torturer") has been subjected to various interpretations. Preceded by the word "sinon" ("if not"), it constitutes the second part of an uncompleted poem, the first part of which the poet had merely outlined in a letter to his publisher Calonne. That this first part had been intended as an ironic commentary on his love for Jeanne, despite his knowledge of her deceit and infidelity, becomes obvious in its summary that he enclosed in the letter: "If you wish to please and renew my desires, be cruel, deceitful, debauched, dissolute, and dishonest; and, if you refuse to be that, I shall strike you senseless."[9]

The poem itself is obviously addressed to one who had offered him her love. It becomes obvious that Baudelaire is referring to himself with the deepest irony and loathing, much as he had done in "Le Vampire," in which he had admitted his powerlessness to break Jeanne's hold over him despite his longing to escape. Believing himself incapable of love that is neither sadistic nor masochistic, he warns the woman to whom the poem is addressed that, if he fails to find in her the torture of love—which he ironically and perversely feels will alone awaken his desires—then he himself will supply that torture and will become both the torturer and the self-tortured. Baudelaire has expressed much the same idea in *Mon Coeur mis à nu*: "As for torture, it is born from the infamous part of man's heart, thirsty for voluptuous pleasure. Cruelty and sensual pleasure are identical, like extreme heat and extreme cold" (OC, I: 683).

The cycle of *Spleen* closes on a note of hopeless despair. In "Irrémédiable," the first eight stanzas consist of a series of powerful images each of which symbolizes the irremediable nature of existence, which Baudelaire views as "Evil." In the darkness of Existence, however, there shines a light, like a beacon—"la conscience dans le Mal."

The final poem, "L'Horloge" ("The Clock"), expresses the poet's realization that even repentance will no longer atone for his procrastination and that the moment is approaching when he will be told that nothing more is left for him in life: "Die, old coward! it is too late."

Tableaux parisiens

In *Le Salon de 1846,* Baudelaire had accused artists of failing to see the poetic and "marvelous" subjects that are to be found everywhere in Parisian life. In *Tableaux parisiens,* which he added to *Les Fleurs du mal* in 1861 and for which he composed ten new poems in addition to the eight moved from *Spleen et Idéal,* the poet has heeded his own advice and created what has been called the cityscape. It is in this section, containing some of his most original poems, that he presents a personal impression of the city and succeeds in extracting what Thibaudet has called "the soul of the city, a subtle, perverse soul, the soul of its nights, the soul of its spleen."[10] Using reality as a point of departure, the poet transforms that reality into something "surnaturel" by the power of his imagination.

In "Paysage" ("Landscape"), the poem that opens the new section, Baudelaire imagines himself in an attic overlooking the city, which he describes in a series of realistic and impressionistic images: a lamp seen in a neighboring window, smoke rising to the sky, "the monotonous snow," and the moon pouring out its "pale enchantment." Despite the cold winter, the poet will be able, through the power of his will (voluntary memory as opposed to the Proustian involuntary memory), to conjure up Springtime and to draw from his heart the warm sunlight of the past.

In many of the poems that follow, Baudelaire continues to combine realistic description with personal impressions. The poet in "Le Soleil" ("The Sun") is likened to the sun, which ennobles even the ugliest object and penetrates both the palace and the hospital. In "A une Mendiante rousse" ("To a Red-Haired Girl"), the poet, adopting a theme made popular in the baroque period, sees in his imagination a thin, sickly, red-haired beggar girl transformed by the rich costumes and the jewels of a sixteenth-century heroine.

"Le Cygne" ("The Swan"), one of Baudelaire's most famous poems, has for its theme a feeling of exile ("in the forest where my spirit is exiled")—a feeling he shares with the many who, like him, have lost what can never be refound. To evoke the sensation of exile, the poet has chosen from the exterior world images that correspond to his feeling of melancoly and nostalgia. As he crosses the new Carrousel, he remembers having seen, during its construction, a swan that had escaped from its cage, dragging its white plumage in the dusty rubble of a waterless stream and gazing at "the ironic and cruelly blue sky" as if reproaching a heartless God. The sight of the pitiful swan awakens other memories: Andromache, exiled from Troy and weeping beside a river which she had had built in imitation of the river Simoïs of her native land; the Negress, thin and consumptive, trudging through the mud and longing for the sight of "la superbe Afrique"; thin and sickly orphans; shipwrecked and forgotten sailors; all those who weep for what has been lost.

The poem is further enhanced by its construction, which has been described as symphonic. The use of the recurring image, the mixture in style resulting from the use of the grand manner and the colloquial style, the quiet, subdued tone—all add to the subtlety of the emotions and help to make it one of Baudelaire's greatest achievements.

Except for the fact that "Les Sept Vieillards" ("The Seven Old Men") and "Les Petites Vieilles" ("Little Old Women") are both concerned with old age and poverty, they have little else in common. Both poems are dedicated to Victor Hugo whom, as Baudelaire admitted in a letter to the poet in exile, he was seeking to emulate. And it was to "Les Sept Vieillards" in particular that Hugo was referring when he answered that Baudelaire had succeeded in creating "un nouveau frisson" ("a new shudder"). Critics have long sought to attach to the seven old men an allegorical meaning, such as the seven capital sins. It seems more likely, however, as Antoine Adam suggests, that the poem is merely one of those hallucinations often experienced by the lonely

"lost in the desert of large cities."[11] Whatever the case, the poem produces a
nightmarish effect by endowing every detail of the city with the ominous
and the menacing.

"Les Petites Vieilles," in contrast to "Les Sept Vieillards," moves from the
sinister and grotesque to what may be called a note of indifferent and detached compassion. There is none of the sentimentality that is sometimes
found in Victor Hugo. Instead, Baudelaire notes the ugliness and decre-
pitude associated with old age: the twisted bodies, the bent back, the mar-
ionette-like movements—"the debris of humanity ripe for eternity." Only
their mysterious eyes, "wells made from millions of tears," have for the poet
"invincible charms" that recall either pools of water shining in the night or
the eyes of a young girl amazed and dazzled by all that glitters and attracts
the eye.

Among the sights that Baudelaire encounters as he traverses the city is
that of the blind ("Les Aveugles"), who stumble along gazing upward with
unseeing eyes. The poem is thought to have been inspired by a reproduction
of a painting by Bruegel depicting the blind who, like sleepwalkers, grope
their way, raising their empty eyes toward heaven, unaware of the deep river
that flows at their feet. Like them, the poet tells us, he too drags himself
along and in even greater bewilderment and despair, asks himself, "What
do all these blind seek in the heavens?" For the poet the heavens are empty,
and his despair is even greater than that of the blind, who seem to believe
that hope may still be within reach.

As he continues his stroll through the city, Baudelaire encounters a lovely
passerby ("A une Passante"), who, as she disappears from sight, brings to
the poet the realization of a love that might have been—"O toi que j'eusse
aimée, O toi qui le savais" ("Oh you, whom I might have loved, oh you,
who knew it"). In gambling dens ("Le Jeu"), he watches greedy, aged gam-
blers and harlots who, to the envious poet, seem actually happier than he in
their choice of "pain to death, and hell to nothingness." And in "Danse Macabre," dedicated to the sculptor Ernest Christophe, he depicts the skeleton
of a woman dressed coquettishly for a ball. Symbolizing the dance of death,
she mingles her irony with the "insanity" of an "unheeding and ludicrous
Humanity." "L'Amour du Mensonge" ("The Love of Lies") reveals
Baudelaire's indifference to stupidity and reaffirms his admiration for
beauty, be it real or merely the result of artifice.

Suddenly, without a transition of any kind, the poet's thoughts revert to
his childhood and, in two poems, the most autobiographical of the entire
volume, he conjures up poignant memories of the past with a warm intensity seldom found in his poetry. The first, beginning "Je n'ai pas oublié" ("I

haven't forgotten"), recalls the childhood days spent with his mother in a small house near the woods of Boulogne, soon after the death of his father. Unlike the poetry of the Romantics, there is almost a complete absence of personal allusions, although the reader is aware of a vague melancholy arising from the impression of solitude and emptiness evoked by the poet. Despite a style that at times verges on the prosaic, the poem, with its quiet reserve and sobriety, and its emphasis on familiar scenes and long-remembered objects, succeeds in evoking "the strange and sad memories" of which he had spoken in a letter of 11 January 1858 to his mother.[12]

The second poem, "La Servante au grand coeur," has been rightly described by Mansell Jones as "a masterpiece of natural pathos . . . whose sweep of vision neither Flaubert nor Verlaine could have approached."[13] Other critics have noted a resemblance to certain lines found in Gautier's "Comédie de la mort." But whereas in Gautier the tirade is purely literary, in Baudelaire's case the poem is based on personal memories and deeply felt emotions, conveyed in a style that mingles the intimate and prosaic with the elevated and eloquent. As in his greatest poems, there are lines that haunt the memory and illustrate the "sorcellerie évocatrice" of which he had spoken in his essay on Gautier.

In "Rêve parisien," Baudelaire sees in a dream a city made from metal and mineral in which there was no light, save that reflected from the objects themselves, and no sound—only the silence of eternity. Nowhere has the poet revealed more clearly his taste for the artificial. The reader is again reminded of his confession in the *Salon de 1859:* "I prefer the monsters of my fantasy to the triviality of reality . . . I find it useless and irksome to represent things as they are" (OC, 2: 620).

Though the dream that he recounts seems to have been induced by drugs (in *Un Mangeur d'Opium* he describes a somewhat similar dream of astonishing and monstrous architecture), it should be remembered that the dream of an artificial world goes back to Novalis and appears rather frequently in Romantic literature, including Poe's "The City in the Sea." Moreover, as Antoine Adam suggests, the poet may also have been inspired by a page in Gautier's *Mlle Maupin* or by his "Une Nuit de Cléopatre."[14] The last two verses constitute a dramatic and unexpected conclusion, as the poet awakens to the sight of his tawdry room and the funereal sound of the clock striking noon.

It is characteristic of Baudelaire that, in his two poems "Crépuscule du soir" ("Twilight") and "Crépuscule du matin" ("Dawn"), he celebrates the city rather than nature. Not that he failed to appreciate the beauty and grandeur of nature, but Baudelaire was above all an anthropocentric poet, interested in man and in man's habitat. In a letter to Desnoyer, who had asked him for some verses on nature, he amusingly expresses his antipathy to Romantic philosophy with its idealistic and pantheistic interpretation of nature: "I am incapable of becoming sentimental about vegetation . . . I consider my own soul of much greater value than that of sanctified vegetables." And he concludes his explanation by adding: "In the depths of the woods, overshadowed by vaults like those of sacristies or cathedrals, I think of our astonishing cities, and the stupendous music that rolls overhead seems to me the translation of human lamentations" (Corr., 1: 248). The two poems that he wrote are indeed the "translation of human lamentation," for in them it is the soul of the city that he sings: its workers, its criminals, its prostitutes, its lonely and its dying.

In "Le Crépuscle du Soir," the poet mingles realism with the "surnaturel" as he describes not so much the city itself as the impression the vices of city life produce in his own soul. The second part of the poem reveals a marked change of tone and becomes a sort of meditation in which the poet reveals his pity for those who suffer and die, and most especially (and here he is evidently thinking of himself) for "those who have never known the sweetness of home and who have never lived."

"Crépuscule du matin" is a masterpiece of its kind in which Baudelaire succeeds in varying the tone by mingling a simple and prosaic style with one that is eloquent, ornate, or lyric. Moreover, like Flaubert, he has succeeded in giving a tragic sense of life to an everyday subject totally lacking in grandeur or sublimity. In his use of realistic detail, he rivals the Realists and, in his comparisons of inanimate objects to animate objects ("the lamp like a bloody eye"), he is using a technique that Zola will later employ in his novels. In the last lines of the poem there is a sudden change of tone as he compares the dawn to a fragile young girl, shivering in her green and rose-colored dress, slowly appearing over the river Seine, while somber Paris, like a tired old laborer, rubs his weary eyes and gathers up his tools in preparation for his long day's work.

In their subjectivity and strange visionary qualities the two poems are reminiscent of the etchings of Méryon, the artist Baudelaire discovered and befriended. Both poet and artist have succeeded in endowing the cityscape with a mysterious and somber spirit. By their use of sinister images (demons bumping against the shutters in Baudelaire; demons and ominous black birds that fill the sky in Méryon) both endow the commonplace with an almost demonic significance and evoke, especially in the case of the poet, the tragedy of human existence.

Le Vin

Having found in the streets and haunts of Paris only his own spleen, Baudelaire, in the 1857 edition, turns to wine as a form of artificial paradise. In the 1861 edition, however, he enlarges his perspective, and wine, symbolizing narcotics in general, becomes for him one of the vices that brings about man's destruction. In this section, entitled *Le Vin,* there are only five poems—poems which are among the most mediocre in the entire volume. "L'Ame du vin" is reminiscent of certain passages found in *Du Vin et du hachisch;* "Le Vin des Chiffonniers" evokes the picturesque figures of the ragpickers who, portrayed by artists including Daumier and Manet, are seen wandering the streets of Paris at night; "Le Vin de l'assassin," an early poem much admired during Baudelaire's lifetime, is a sort of crude poetic drama that lacks the evocative magic of his best work. The two last poems, "Le Vin du solitaire" and "Le Vin des amants," complete the section. Of them, the latter with its vision of escape into a paradise of dreams recalls poems such as "Elévation" and "Moesta et Errabunda."

Fleurs du mal

In the 1857 edition of *Les Fleurs du mal,* the cycle entitled *Fleurs du mal* followed that of *Spleen et Idéal.* By changing its position in 1861 and by placing it after *Le Vin,* Baudelaire seems to suggest that the experiences he describes are another desperate but failed attempt to escape the dreaded sensation of *Ennui.* The intention of the opening poem, "La Destruction," becomes more clear if the reader looks back to "Au Lecteur" in which Baudelaire had maintained that *ennui* is the greatest of our vices ("he dreams of scaffolds while smoking his *houka*"). In fact, Baudelaire is confirming what he had already said in the opening poem. By indulging in sadistic dreams—dreams of torture, of destruction, of violence—he is seeking to stimulate and bring back to life his deadened emotions and his exhausted nerves.

Equally important is the fact that the poem was originally entitled "Volupté," an allusion to Sainte-Beuve's novel *Volupté,* much admired by Baudelaire, in which the protagonist Amaury is caught in a struggle between his gross sensuality and his more spiritual longings. This is precisely the theme of "La Destruction" in which, as Antoine Adam suggests, man, crazed by *ennui* and seeking to awaken his sensibilities, finally discovers the means of doing so in the joy of destruction.[15]

Throughout the rest of the cycle Baudelaire continues to emphasize the deceptive charm of evil and its disastrous consequences. In "Les Deux Bonnes Soeurs" ("The Two Good Sisters"), Death is identified as the sister of Debauchery and the inevitable consequence of evil. In "La Fontaine de sang," the poet sees his own destruction in the sight of his blood pouring in an endless stream from an unseen wound. It may be that in this early poem Baudelaire was thinking of his association with Louchette from whom he had contracted the disease that was to destroy his health and to result indirectly in his death. "Allégorie" celebrates the amoral woman who fearlessly faces death without either hate or remorse, whereas "La Béatrix" who, like Dante's Beatrice, had once served the poet as a source of inspiration, has now joined his enemies in mocking and deriding him.

In his essay on Gautier, Baudelaire had expressed his belief that "the horrible artistically expressed becomes beauty" (*OC,* 1:123). The poet seems to have done just that in "Une Martyre." In no other poem has he mingled so effectively dramatic and pictorial power: the calm and sumptious beauty of an ornate room redolent with the scent of decaying flowers, and the sight of a woman's decapitated body, naked except for one stocking, her head set apart on a small night table. Once again, Baudelaire associates love and evil with the horror of death as he reenacts in his imagination the circumstances of the murder and the violation of the corpse.

It is only in the poems on lesbianism that Baudelaire introduces a note of compassion, though in "Delphine et Hippolyte," one of the condemned poems, he concludes with a violent denunciation of their sin. "Femmes damnées," which escaped being banned in 1857, is evidence of this compassion in its sympathy for those who ignore custom and social law. "Less voluptuous than pensive," as Prévost suggests, it fails to condemn, and expresses only pity for the "chercheuses d'infini" ("Seekers of the Infinite") who suffer as much torment as pleasure in their desperate quest for happiness.[16]

"Femmes damnées—Delphine et Hippolyte" comes closest to eroticism but to an eroticism which is made neither inviting nor pleasurable. Called by Vivier a "miniature drama," it contains some of Baudelaire's finest imagery as in his comparison of Delphine's kisses to the caressing touch of a moth hovering over a large, transparent lake.[17] In sharp contrast to the preceding stanzas, the poem ends with a thundering moral indictment that is overly rhetorical in its furious condemnation of "the lamentable victims" doomed to eternal perdition.

"Lesbos," which originally preceded the two poems entitled "Femmes damnées" and which was also banned by the courts, looks back almost nostalgically to a time long since past, when Sappho "more beautiful than

Venus," having defied the "rites" by giving herself to a man, "died the day of her blasphemy." More melancholy than erotic, it appeals mainly to our poetic emotions and concludes on a note of sadness made more nostalgic and songlike by its effective use of refrains that introduce and close each stanza.

"Un Voyage à Cythère," the finest of the poems that constitute the cycle of *Fleurs du mal,* is, as Baudelaire states in the penultimate stanza, an "allegory" suffused with the irony and "surnaturalisme" which he had once characterized as "two fundamental literary qualities" (*OC,* 1:658).

The theme is not only a criticism directed at Baudelaire himself but also an ironic commentary on the idealized love portrayed by the Romantics. Together with the poet, the reader discovers that the legendary Cythera, "a beautiful island covered with green myrtles," was in reality only a "rocky desert disturbed by sharp cries." Moreover, that which he had first thought to be a temple near which a young priestess walked, her dress half opening in the breeze, was in reality a three-forked gallows from which hung a blackened corpse being devoured by ravenous birds.

Recognizing that the hanged was an inhabitant of Cythera expiating his infamous sins, Baudelaire identifies himself with the victim. In a strange admixture of styles, so characteristic of the poet, he mingles a crude image ("vomit mounting to my teeth") with the more poetic conclusion: "Oh Lord, give me the strength and the courage to contemplate my heart and my body without disgust." Moreover, here, as elsewhere in his poetry, he succeeds brilliantly in his use of concrete images to express both sensations and emotions.

The cycle of *Fleurs du mal* concludes with a short poem based on an engraving by Hendrik Goltzius (1558–1617) in which Cupid, seated on a skull, is blowing bubbles. That it was intended to be another example of destruction through sexual vice is made clear by the vain protests of the skull: "What your cruel mouth scatters in the air . . . is my brain, my blood, and my flesh."

Revolt

After seeking in vain to escape his ennui in wine and in evil, Baudelaire rejects his illusions and finds solace in a revolt against an imperfect world—a world "where action is [not] the sister of the dream." The sentiment expressed in the opening quatrains of "Le Reniement de Saint Pierre," in which he denounces the sadistic pleasure and malevolence of a cruel God in the face of suffering humanity, was a commonplace in Romantic literature. But where Lamartine, Vigny, Gautier, and Nerval directed their attacks at God, it is Christ that Baudelaire rejects, and for the very reasons cited by Proudhon in both his *Carnets* and his other works.

The poet's denial of Christ is based neither on hate nor on fear. On the contrary, while admitting Christ's divinity and remembering his suffering and crucifixion, he speaks to him with a note of tenderness and sorrowful reproach. It is not Christ himself that the poet denounces; it was rather Christ's failure to seek reform through positive action. If pain and evil are to be destroyed, man must be encouraged to struggle—"to fight and to die by the sword." Rather than submit, Christ should have remained master and should have continued his efforts to combat evil.[18]

The theme was one that Proudhon had stressed throughout his life, and Baudelaire was well acquainted both with the social reformer and with his works. It was no coincidence that the poet chose as the title of his poem "Le Reniement [Denial] de Saint-Pierre." A passage in Proudhon's *Carnets,* in which the social reformer likewise rejects Christ, begins with the very theme of Baudelaire's poem: "As for me, I *deny* you, and I shall burn your Gospel" (italics added).[19]

Like "Le Reniement de Saint Pierre," "Abel et Caïn" also reflects the thought and influence of Proudhon. Abel symbolizes a rich, smug society, content with its lot; Cain, on the other hand, symbolizes the proletariat struggling to exist. A rebel who rejects both society and an unjust and cruel God, Cain is urged by the poet to revolt and to cast down upon the earth God himself. The poem seems only another way of expressing the frenzied virulence characteristic of Proudhon: "God is stupidity and cowardice; God is hypocrisy and a lie; God is tyranny and poverty; God is evil."[20]

"Les Litanies de Satan," inspired and based on the "Miserere" of the Catholic liturgy, is an incantatory poem composed of fifteen stanzas, each of which numbers only two lines and is followed by a one-line refrain. The poem concludes with a prayer of six lines addressed to Satan. This is not the Satan of whom Baudelaire spoke in "Au Lecteur" and in his letter to Flaubert. Nor is it the Satan of the two postulations. On the contrary, this is the Satan of the Romantics, who had adopted Milton's Lucifer as a symbol of revolt and of heroic energy—a Satan who, in the form of protagonists like Schiller's Karl Moor, Byron's Cain, or Balzac's Vautrin, revolts against the injustice of the social order as well as against the cruelty of God and of nature.

An early poem, it conforms to the revolutionary sentiments of Proudhon and the Baudelaire of 1848: God is evil, Christ has failed; Satan, having suffered defeat in silence, remains man's only comforter. It is he who offers suffering humanity its only hope—that of open revolt against an oppressive government and a cruel society.

Cycle of Death

The cycle of Death, which contained only three poems in the 1857 edition, was increased to six in 1861. Its five sonnets are followed by "Le Voyage," the longest and perhaps greatest of his poems. The loveliest and most perfect of the sonnets is "L'Amour des amants," noted for its melodious beauty, which inspired both Debussy and Villiers de l'Isle-Adam to set it to music. In "La Mort des Pauvres" death is welcomed as the only hope and the only goal in life, for it is an entry into a new life, a gate that opens onto "unknown heavens." As for those artists ("La Mort des artistes") who have never really known their idol, "death soaring like a new sun" will bring to fruition the dreams they have but vaguely glimpsed.

Written in 1859 when Baudelaire was visiting his mother in Honfleur in the charming Maison-Joujou overlooking the sea, "Le Voyage" brings *Les Fleurs du mal* to its logical conclusion. In it, he reintroduces the important themes he had treated throughout the volume: the taste for the infinite, the desire to escape, the quest for the unknown, the prevalence of sin, disbelief in progress, time viewed as man's enemy, and a longing for the unknown.

Despite its division into eight sections, the internal structure of the poem is comparatively simple. It begins with the evocation of a small child poring over maps and prints in the lamplight and marveling at the immensity of the universe—a universe that in the eyes of memory will appear to be far smaller than he had believed.

In the verses that follow, the poet describes a group of travelers about to set sail—some to dispel their ennui, others to forget disappointment in love, and still others ("the real travelers") to seek "unknown" pleasures in their quest for the ideal. But the travelers meet only with disappointment, and to their curious friends who, on their return, question them about their experiences, they admit that everywhere they had found only the "tedious spectacle of immortal sin." For the poet there remains still another voyage, a final voyage with Death as its captain. And in lines marked by an almost joyous expectation, the poet calls on Death to set sail, regardless of the destination, be it Heaven or Hell. Weary of life, he has lost all but one desperate hope— that of discovering in death something other than the hideous torture he had known in life and of finding "in the depths of the unknown something *new.*"

Stylistically, Baudelaire has perhaps never succeeded more brilliantly: the dramatic use of dialogue and monologue; the change of tone from casual to the sweeping eloquence of the grand manner; references to the distant past that enlarge the scope of the poem and open up new horizons; alternations in mood from the somber and ironic to the joyous and exalted. Imagery, in particular, is strikingly original and suggestive: our soul as a three-master seeking its Icaria; imagination as a drunken sailor stumbling in the mud and dreaming of paradise; imagination as an old tree whose branches seek to see the sun more closely. Throughout it all Baudelaire has succeeded in overcoming despair by the very imagination with which he had evoked that despair. And the poem closes on a note of triumph that verges on bravado.

"Le Voyage" was not Baudelaire's final view of approaching death. In 1861 there appeared in *Le Parnasse contemporain* a group of poems that were later to be included in the 1868 edition of *Les Fleurs du mal*. Among them is to be found one of Baudelaire's most beautiful and poignant poems, entitled "Recueillement," whose very simplicity strangely defies translation. Perhaps no better example can be found of the poet's belief that "it is one of the prodigious privileges of art . . . that *sorrow*, given rhythm and cadence, fills the mind with a calm *joy*" (*OC*, 2:123).

It is only after reading the entire poem that the reader discovers that "Recueillement" is actually a symbolic poem, that the poet is speaking *not* of the coming night, but rather of coming death. In his loneliness and isolation he finds no one in whom he may confide and, turning to his grief, he addresses it, as if it were a small child, with the tender, intimate, and coaxing words of a child's world.

The quiet tenderness and haunting simplicity of the first lines are followed by the broken phrasing of the third line, which seems to suggest the breathless waiting of the poet and the child. Suddenly the rhythm becomes more sweeping as the poet notes the slow approach of night that comes to appease the torments of a lonely soul. After a long, subordinate clause depicting the clamor of the city, Baudelaire resumes the intimate personal note only to return to the use of allegory, as he sees in his imagination the dead years dressed in old-fashioned gowns, leaning over the balcony, Regret rising from the depths of the water, and the Sun falling asleep under the arch of the bridge. There follow two of the loveliest lines to be found in all of Baudelaire's poetry: "Et, comme un long linceul traînant à l'Orient / Entends, ma chère, entends la douce Nuit qui marche" ("And like a long shroud trailing in the East / Listen, my dear, to the footfalls of the gentle Night").

Although Valéry has criticized lines five to seven as being "incontestably weak," other critics, notably Michael Riffaterre, have wisely noted the need for the contrast that only emphasizes the simplicity and the poignancy of the lines that follow.[21] There seems little doubt that "Recueillement" reveals a change of heart from that expressed in "Le Voyage." Triumph and willpower have yielded to quiet acceptance and to a willingness to welcome Death, which is now viewed as a "gentle night" that alone can bring comfort to a weary and desolate heart.

Chapter Five

Petits Poèmes en prose, or Le Spleen de Paris

Inspired by Aloyius Bertrand's *Gaspard de la nuit* (1842), which had been edited and prefaced by Sainte-Beuve, Baudelaire's prose poems, known today as *Le Spleen de Paris,* were an attempt not only to extract beauty from modern daily life, but also to endow that life with symbolic meaning. Whereas Bertrand, in accord with the taste of the Romanticists for the picturesque and the extraordinary, had written about the Dijon of the Middle Ages, Baudelaire sought his inspiration in the everyday world of contemporary Paris—in its crowds, its fairs, its street scenes, its beauty and mystery.

And yet, the city of Paris itself, though never mentioned by name, plays a smaller part in the volume than one might expect, despite the epilogue dedicated to the "capitale infame." Moreover, whenever it serves as a background for a particular poem, it is not the picturesque character of the city that Baudelaire evokes. On the contrary, he makes no effort to differentiate its topographical aspects, nor does he ever identify it other than by the expression "ville énorme."

What Baudelaire attempts above all is to "lay bare," as Thibaudet once wrote, not only "*a* soul in a large city," but also "*the* soul of a large city" [italics added].[1] He longed to find universal communion with the crowds, especially with those individuals who, like himself, lonely and misunderstood, wished to "bathe themselves" in the multitude. For them, *Le Spleen de Paris* was perfectly appropriate as a title. But for those poems which have nothing to do with city life, it was much less fitting. It was obviously this fact that explains Baudelaire's frequent changes of title, as well as his tendency to resort to using *Petits Poèmes en prose* as a sort of generic title.

The poet first adopted the title *Le Spleen de Paris* in his letters of March 1863 and, although he abandoned it on occasion, it is the one to which he refers in a letter written several days before his first serious attack of illness in 1866. Its choice has been justified in recent years by Claude Pichois, who suggests that the collection of prose poems may be thought of as "marked by a Parisian and modern spirit, no matter how exotic or foreign to Paris they may be" (*OC*,1:1300).

Unlike *Les Fleurs du mal, Le Spleen de Paris* is lacking in unity or in any qualities that may be viewed as architectural. In fact, in the dedication to Arsène Houssaye that precedes the twenty poems published in *La Presse* in September 1862, Baudelaire stresses this very lack of architectural unity: "If you remove a vertebra, the two pieces of this tortuous caprice would unite without difficulty. Break it into many pieces, and you will see that each can exist by itself" (*OC*,1:275).

The poet himself thought of the prose poems as "un pendant," a companion piece, to *Les Fleurs du mal*. In a letter written 19 February 1866 to Jules Troubat, Sainte-Beuve's secretary, he even described them as "another *Les Fleurs du mal* but with much more freedom and detail and raillery" (*Corr.*, 2:615). Like *Tableaux parisiens,* the prose poems were obviously an attempt to prove, in part at least, what he had written in *Le Salon de 1846*: "Parisian life is rich in poetic and marvelous subjects. The marvelous envelops us and steeps us like the atmosphere; but we do not see it" (*OC*, 2:496). And so in the prose poems we note even more clearly than in the *Tableaux parisiens* the spectacle of elegant life and "the thousands of stray souls who move about in the underworld of a great city. . . ." (*OC*, 2:495).

There is little doubt that the use of prose made it easier for the poet to utilize both modern and urban subjects and also to combine, as he wrote to his mother on 9 March 1865, "the terrifying with the comic, and even love with hate" (*Corr.,* 2:473). Not that he had failed to do just that in certain poems of *Les Fleurs du mal*—but there is little doubt that it was easier to introduce into prose various tones such as irony, sarcasm, and cruelty without diminishing the poetic effect.

In many of his prose poems Baudelaire was actually doing what he maintained Daumier had succeeded in accomplishing: "You will see passing before your eyes all that a great city contains of living monstrosities—all that it harbors of the fearful, the grotesque, the sinister or the farcical" (*OC,* 2:554). Baudelaire could well have been describing certain of his own prose poems, some of which were actually inspired by the great caricaturist. There is little doubt, as Lemaitre has shown, that the art of Daumier, Guys, and Méryon, as well as the stories of Edgar Allan Poe, did much to encourage and inspire in Baudelaire the mingling of the strange and commonplace.[2] In fact, Baudelaire came to believe that modern beauty could be born only from this intimate association of the two contrasting elements.

To Sainte-Beuve he wrote on 4 May 1865: "To produce a *hundred* laborious trifles—a strange excitation which has need of spectators, crowds,

music, even gaslights—that's what I have wanted to do!" (*Corr.*, 2:493).
And the following year, 15 January 1866, he describes in more precise
terms the actual format of the poems: "At last, I hope that one of these days
I can show a new Joseph Delorme coupling his rhapsodic thought to each
incident of his walks while drawing from each object a disagreeable moral"
(*Corr.*, 2:583).[3]

Of the hundred poems Baudelaire told Sainte-Beuve he had intended to
write, only fifty appear in the posthumous edition. And from his letters we
know that the fifty were composed under the most harrowing circumstances. Though he had written Jules Troubat on 19 February 1866 that he
was finishing the last pages of the projected volume, less than a month later
(5 March 1866) he complained in still another letter: "Ah! this *Spleen,* what
fits of anger and what work it has caused me! And I am still dissatisfied
with certain parts" (*Corr.*, 2:627).

Knowing Baudelaire's physical condition during his years in Brussels—
his violent spells of dizziness and nausea, his inability at times to leave his
room or even his bed—it seems almost a miracle that he accomplished as
much as he did. To his mother he confessed in a letter of 4 May 1865 that
he had fallen into a real depression and that he lacked the courage to work
on his *Poèmes en prose.* And to his friend Manet a few days later he was even
more explicit: "As for finishing *Pauvre Belgique,* I am incapable; I am too
exhausted, I am dead. I have a number of *Poèmes en prose* to send to two or
three journals. But I can't do any more" (*Corr.*, 2:497).

Baudelaire was not exaggerating. His friend Poulet-Malassis, who had
escaped debtor's prison by taking refuge in Belgium and who had been one
of the few to bring a glimmer of happiness into Baudelaire's life in Belgium,
became increasingly aware of the poet's physical and mental deterioration.
"His intermittent intellectual powerlessness which he must often have mentioned to you, as he has to me, has become continuous, or almost so," he
wrote to Asselineau in 1866.[4] It is hardly surprising then that the poet's deteriorating health is sometimes reflected in his work, and that, as a consequence, the poems are of unequal quality.

Baudelaire's early prose poems had their source in his verse poems. In
1857, three of the six published poems ("Le Crèpuscule du soir," "Un
Hémisphère dans une chevelure," and "L'Invitation au voyage") have their
counterparts in *Les Fleurs du mal.* In 1861, the prose poem "Les Veuves"
("Widows") dealt with much the same theme as "Les Petites Vieilles" ("Little Old Women"). And "A une Heure du matin" ("One O'clock in the
Morning") and "La belle Dorothée" are merely prose versions of "L'Examen
du minuit" and "Bien loin d'ici" ("Very far from here"). Still others are

based on notations found in his *Journaux intimes:* "La Fausse Monnaie" ("The Fake Coin"), "Perte d'auréole" ("Loss of a halo"), and "Le Galant Tireur" ("The Galant Marksman").

Later Baudelaire enlarged the scope and variety of his prose poems by introducing themes that he developed at greater length. In all, he not only serves as narrator, but also assumes the role of participant or observer, and in some cases that of all three. Regardless of the format, the poet unfailingly reveals aspects of his own complex personality or presents some philosophical or psychological truth that explains either his own actions or those of persons he has closely observed.

Underlying most of the themes, and sometimes serving as the theme itself, is the feeling of solitude versus multitude enunciated in two poems entitled "Les Foules" ("Crowds") and "La Solitude." Though the poet longs to find a sort of "universal communion" with the crowds in the streets, he remains ever conscious of his solitude, unable or unwilling to abolish the limits that separate him from others. In a letter to Sainte-Beuve of 4 May 1865 expressing his difficulty in composing his prose poems, he remarks: "I need that *bath in the multitude* whose inaccuracy rightly shocked you" (*Corr.,* 2:493). Perhaps the poet was remembering his many walks through the streets of Paris with Constantin Guys and the artist's scornful remark: "Any man . . . who *gets bored in the midst of the crowd is an* idiot! An idiot! and I have only the greatest contempt for him" (*OC,* 2:692).

Yet Baudelaire was also perfectly aware of the possibility of enjoying solitude, whether alone or in the very midst of the crowd. "He who cannot people his solitude doesn't know how to be alone in a busy crowd," he wrote in *Les Foules.* "It is the poet especially," he continues, "who enjoys the incomparable priviledge of being, at will, himself or another." "Solitude," he notes in the poem by that title, "is dangerous only for the idle and rambling soul who peoples it with his passions and his imaginings."

As for the subject matter, Baudelaire has made no attempt to group the poems according to themes, or even to formulate a pattern of any kind. Some are of urban inspiration, usually anecdotal in character; others are lyrical outbursts or quiet meditations—reveries marked by an absence of plot or intrigue. Many, no longer than one or two paragraphs, express an idea or voice a personal emotion. A few are actually short stories reminiscent of Edgar Allan Poe. All have about them the same confessional qualities that characterize the *Journaux intimes.* In fact, as we have seen, many are only the further development of an observation already recorded in his journal. Most either begin or conclude with what Baudelaire had described to Sainte-Beuve as a "morale désagréable"—a statement that assumes the form of a maxim or of a psychological, moral, or philosophical truth discerned by the poet in even the most trivial incidents and sights encountered by him in the city streets.

Baudelaire's tendency to reveal certain aspects of his own personality in his prose poems is particularly evident in *Les Vocations,* where four small boys, all of whom prefigure the poet, discuss their future vocations. In each case Baudelaire is looking back on his own childhood dreams and ambitions, which in later life become subjects of both his poetry and prose. The first child, who wishes to emulate the actors of a theatrical performance he had once seen, has already been met in *Mon Coeur mis à nu:* "As a child, I wanted at times to be a pope, but a military pope, at other times an actor" (*OC,* 1:702).

The second child, who sees God on a beautiful white cloud, has been introduced to us in the *Journaux intimes:* "From my childhood, tendency to mysticism. My conversations with God" (*OC,* 1:706). The third child who, on having been obliged to spend a night in the family maid's bed recalls the smoothness of her skin and the perfume of her luxuriant hair, reveals the eroticism of the older Baudelaire, whereas the fourth boy, on hearing the wildly passionate music of a group of gypsies whom he longs to join in their wandering Bohemian existence, recalls another notation in the *Journaux intimes:* "To glorify vagabondage and what is called Bohemianism, cult of multiple sensation, expressing itself through music" (*OC,* 1:701).

The tone of the opening poem, "L'Etranger," is in complete contrast to the thundering rhetoric of "Au Lecteur" ("To the Reader") in *Les Fleurs du mal.* In the simplest of dialogues—a series of questions and answers exchanged between two strangers—the poet evokes the sense of solitude that seems to have haunted him since childhood. We have only to remember his notation in *Mon Coeur mis à nu:* "Feeling of *solitude* from my childhood . . . feeling of an eternally solitary destiny" (*OC,* 1:680).

In "L'Etranger" the artist is still a "loner," the dandy who seeks escape from spleen in the beauty of nature as revealed in the movement of the clouds. This is the same person who, enthralled by the beauty of Boudin's cloud paintings, had remarked in *Le Salon de 1859:* "Strangely enough, not even once did I happen to complain of the absence of man while examining those liquid or aerial enchantments" (*OC,* 2:666).

The same feeling of escapism, of the desire to enjoy in solitude the beauty of sky and sea is to be found in the poem "Déjà" ("Already"). Here the poet, alone among the joyous passengers, is saddened at the thought of "bidding farewell" to the incomparable beauty of the sea that seems to him to contain "the agony and the ecstacy of all the souls who have lived, who live, and who will live." Yet his sorrow is somewhat counterbalanced by the thought of a "rich and magnificent land, full of promise, which was sending forth a mysterious perfume of rose and musk and from which the music of life was coming to reach them in an amorous murmur."

Like "L'Etranger" and "Déjà," "Le Port" is a short commentary on "the mysterious and aristocratic pleasure" derived from the sight of a busy port, as seen by the solitary and aloof poet "weary of life's struggles." His fascination with the magnificence of an ever-changing sky and sea, and his unspoken but obvious scorn for those who, like him, still have the desire and strength to travel or grow rich, reveal two different aspects of his own temperament. In the face of nature, his attitude is that of the solitary aesthete; in the face of the travelers, it becomes that of the dandy "who does nothing," as he had written in his *Journaux intimes* (*OC*, 1:682).

The feeling of solitude prevalent throughout the prose poems is even more apparent in "Les Fenêtres" ("Windows"), in which the poet describes a scene reminiscent of one of Méryon's most famous and dramatic prints, *The Morgue*. In Méryon's somber etching, the mysterious windows of the tenement adjoining the morgue—some the blackest of black, others still brightly lit behind drawn shades—recall "the black or luminous holes" of "Les Fenêtres" behind which "life lives, life dreams, life suffers." To the reader who may question the plausibility of Baudelaire's imaginary account of the scene transpiring behind one of the drawn shades—that of a poor, wrinkled, prematurely old woman, bent over her work—the poet answers simply: "What matters the reality outside myself, if it has helped me to live, to feel who I am and what I am?" In other words, the window has become, as Hiddleston suggests, the perfect symbol, "bringing together inside and outside, dream and reality, self and non-self, and the spectacle, thus perceived, becomes for the poet a means of self-exploration."[5]

Nowhere is Baudelaire's desire for escape made more obvious than in "N'importe où hors du Monde" ("Anywhere out of the World"). To his soul longing for escape from its habitat, the narrator (Baudelaire himself) offers one enticing suggestion after another. Finally, in exasperation at the narrator's futile suggestions and at his lack of understanding, the soul cries out in a burst of rage: "Anywhere! Anywhere, provided it is out of this world."

Solitude coupled with rejection is strikingly evoked in the prose poem "Le Désespoir de la vieille" in which the poet describes the despair of an old woman whose decrepit appearance so frightens the child she wishes to caress that he screams and struggles in terror. Withdrawn "into her eternal solitude," she weeps quietly at the thought that time's havoc has brought horror even to the small children she longs to offer her love.

It is possible that once again Baudelaire found his inspiration for this prose poem in art, as Lemaitre suggests; a Daumier drawing that was approximately contemporaneous with the poem not only treats the same subject but is even entitled *La Vieille Femme et l'enfant*.[6]

Solitude is again the subject of one of Baudelaire's finest and longest prose poems, "Les Veuves," in which he evokes the image of a solitary widow who, evidently too poor to pay the price of admission, is seated at a distance from the well-dressed crowd attending a concert in the park. Her dignity, her aloof and aristocratic beauty, and the sorrowful expression in her eyes that attracts and fascinates the poet are suddenly explained by the sight of her widow's garb and the small boy, also dressed in black, whom she holds by the hand as she listens in rapt attention to the music being played in the distance. That "Les Veuves" is exactly contemporaneous (1861) with Manet's famous painting, *La Musique aux Tuileries,* and contains a description of the crowd that corresponds strikingly to the painting is explained by Baudelaire's close friendship with the artist, whom he accompanied daily to the Tuileries Gardens while the painting was in progress.

Even more interesting is the fact that a wash drawing by Constantin Guys, entitled *Aux Champs-Elysées,* was actually one of the principal sources of Manet's painting and indirectly that of Baudelaire's prose poem. The fact that Baudelaire actually owned the wash drawing, that Manet saw it in the poet's apartment, as well as the common knowledge that Manet often borrowed ideas from old masters (in this case, however, a contemporary artist) all lend credence to the belief that Baudelaire and Manet were indebted to Guys for their choice of subject matter.[7] But whereas Manet was interested only in the glittering crowd, Baudelaire returns to the theme of solitude versus multitude, giving it even greater poignancy by contrasting the widow's loneliness and isolation with that of the carefree and happy audience gathered together in the park.

One of the most moving of the prose poems that expresses sympathy for the solitude of the poor and rejected is "Le Vieux Saltimbanque" ("The Old Clown"), so reminiscent of Daumier's magnificent clown portrayals, most of which were done in the late 1850s or the early 1860s. Before leaving for Brussels in 1864, Baudelaire must surely have seen some of the final versions or, at the very least, some of the many preparatory drawings kept by the artist in a number of notebooks.

Published 1 November 1861 in the *Revue fantaisiste,* "Le Vieux Saltimbanque" has much in common with Daumier's watercolor *The Side*

Show, in which an old clown, worn and decrepit, standing alone outside his hut, vainly beats his drum in hope of attracting the boisterous crowd seen in the distance, laughing and enjoying the antics of other more popular performers. In the poet's version, the old clown has given up in despair: "The poor wretch didn't laugh! He didn't weep, he didn't dance, he didn't gesticulate, he didn't cry out; he sang no song, either gay or sad, he didn't implore. He was mute and motionless. He had given up, he had abdicated. His destiny was made."

Baudelaire, who serves as both narrator and participant, decides to take his leave, but is swept away by a passing crowd before he has an opportunity to place a few coins on one of the benches. To himself he admits having recognized in the clown the image of an old man of letters who had outlived his time and who "without friends, without family, without children, degraded by poverty and public ingratitude, and in whose hut the forgetful world no longer wishes to enter." The reader is reminded of the poet's letter to his mother of 11 September 1856: "I saw before me an interminable succession of years without a family, without friends, without a mistress, endless years of loneliness and troubles and nothing to fill my heart" (*Corr.,* 1:356).

In "A une Heure du matin" (At One O'clock in the Morning"), Baudelaire finds in the silence of the night the solitude he now craves and that he hopes will free him temporarily from "the tyranny of the human face." Combined with the theme of solitude is that of the redemptive dignity of art to which the poet gives expression in his despairing prayer: "Lord, my God! grant me the grace of producing some beautiful verses which may prove to me that I am not the last of men and that I am not inferior to those I scorn."

Critics have pointed out the similarity of the prayer to that of the Pharisee in the Gospel of Luke: "Lord, I thank thee that I am not as other men are, extortioners, unjust, adulterers, or even as this publican." It should be noted, however, that Baudelaire, unlike the Pharisee, is not thanking God because he *is* a good poet. On the contrary, he is asking God to help him *become* such a poet if only to prove to himself that he is not the last of men and that he is not inferior to those for whom he feels only scorn. It is a prayer that arises out of his own self-doubts and self-hatred—a prayer, completely lacking in hypocrisy, whose sentiments every great artist must have felt in his heart in moments of doubt or despair.

Some of Baudelaire's most effective prose poems are those concerned with social injustice—those that express a genuine compassion for the poor, the misfits, and for all those who have been rejected by society. One of the most compelling, "Les Yeux des pauvres" ("The Eyes of the Poor") not only reveals a sense of genuine pity on the part of the author, but also reflects his contempt for the vain and heartless woman who fails to share or even comprehend his feeling of compassion.

Again acting as both narrator and participant, Baudelaire is deeply moved by the sight of a poverty-stricken family—a father and his shabbily dressed children—who, standing before the lighted window of a restaurant, gaze in rapt astonishment at the garish decor and the lavish display of food. Moved by the pathos of the scene, the poet turns to his companion to share with her his emotion, only to discover her irritation at the sight of those "unbearable people with eyes as big as saucers" whom no one bothers to drive away. More than by her heartlessness, the poet is struck by the "incommunicability" that exists even among those in love.

The question of social and economic injustice is again raised in the prose poem "Assommons les pauvres" ("Let Us Beat the Poor"). On noting the title the reader expects to find Baudelaire's attitude toward the poor to be one of heartlessness, if not of sadism. After actually reading the poem, however, the reader discovers that the title is only another example of the "titre pétard" of which Baudelaire was so fond.

There is no question that "Assommons les pauvres" was inspired by ideas of Proudhon; for at the bottom of the manuscript copy Baudelaire had written: "What do you say to this, Proudhon?" Although most critics maintain that the poem is a repudiation of Proudhon's theories, it should be noted that Baudelaire, like the social reformer, rejects pity and Christian charity as ineffectual and demeaning, whereas "the *good* Demon" who inspires the poet to beat the beggar who approaches him is referred to as a "Demon of *action*," reminiscent of the poem "Le Reniement de St. Pierre," in which "action" is described as "the sister of the dream" [italics added].

If Baudelaire beats the beggar, it is not through any evil impulse; it is rather a means of restoring the man's dignity and pride. "You are now my equal," he tells the beggar afterward and, offering to share his purse with him, advises the beggar to follow his example under similar circumstances. Moreover, it is important to note that the beggar understands and agrees to adopt the same theory.[8]

If there is any difference between Proudhon's ideas and those of Baudelaire—and that difference would be slight—it would be the fact that the social reformer puts all the blame on the inequities of the social system whereas the poet, under the influence of de Maistre and Poe, attributes part of the blame to the individual himself.[9] He would no doubt have seen much truth in Shakespeare's lines: "The fault, dear Brutus, lies not in our stars, but in ourselves that we are underlings."

Among the poems dealing with the question of social injustice—of the poor versus the rich—is one known as "Le Joujou du pauvre" ("The Poor Child's Toy"). It portrays two children gazing at each other through a fence separating a large, well-kept estate from a dusty road bordered by thistles and nettles.

Within the fence a well-dressed child, who has cast aside his expensive toy, is eyeing with rapt attention a small puny child who stands in the road, carrying with him as his only toy a live rat locked in a cage. As the two stare at each other through the fence—a symbol of the barrier separating the world of the rich from that of the poor—they smile "fraternally" with teeth of an "egalitarian" whiteness. The poem smacks of the doctrine of Proudhon and of his concern for the social and economic injustice of the day. Whatever the case, the ironic commentary with which the poem is concluded seems too lacking in subtlety, too closely related to political propaganda to be aesthetically effective. The poet seems to have forgotten the observation made in his essay on *Madame Bovary:* "The logic of the work satisfies all the claims of morality, and it is for the reader to draw his conclusions from the conclusion" (*OC,* 2:81–82).

It was this same concern with social and economic injustice, coupled with his own firm belief in original sin, that prompted Baudelaire to write "Le Gâteau." While the poet-narrator wanders through a landscape whose grandeur had almost convinced him to accept Rousseau's idea of "the natural goodness of man"—a concept he had long derided—he witnesses an incident whose brutality appeared in strong contrast to the beauty of the scene.[10]

Suddenly, while he was enjoying his lunch, a small boy appeared, "ragged, grimy, disheveled," who seemed to be devouring with "eyes that were sunken, timid and pleading," the bread that "in a low, hoarse voice" he referred to as "cake." When the narrator, seized by pity, offered him the slice of bread, there appeared, as if out of nowhere, another small boy equally pathetic in appearance.

The sight of the vicious and violent struggle that ensued over the piece of bread, which was soon reduced to a mass of worthless crumbs, saddened the narrator and caused him to conclude, "There is then a superb country in which bread is called *cake,* a delicacy so rare that it is enough to cause a war that is entirely fratricidal." This conclusion belies those critics who maintain that Baudelaire's irony is directed at the "monstruosité" of the child of which the poet speaks in *Le Salon de 1859.* It was far more likely to have

been inspired by Proudhon's *Philosophie de la misère,* in which the social reformer views poverty as the result of the existing social and economic injustice allowed to exist in a country that in this case was otherwise known to be
"superb."[11]

One of the themes, whether primary or secondary, that keeps recurring in
the prose poems is Baudelaire's ambivalent attitude toward women, already
explored in "Les Yeux des pauvres." The love-hate relationship and the feeling of incommunicability that exists between man and wife, or man and
mistress, assumes a sadistic tone in "Le Galant Tireur" ("The Gallant
Marksman") in which the husband, in order to kill "Time," visits a shooting
gallery, accompanied by his "delicious and execrable wife, the mysterious
woman to whom he owes so many pleasures, so many sorrows, and perhaps
also a large part of his *genius*" [italics added].

In the shooting gallery, Baudelaire continues to insist on the ambivalence
of the husband's emotions. As he takes aim at the doll-like figure, he turns
to his companion and announces: "My dear angel, *I am imagining that it is
you.*" Having succeeded in decapitating the doll, he turns once again "to his
dear, his delicious, his execrable wife, his inevitable and pitiless Muse," and,
kissing her hand, adds ironically, "Ah, my dear angel, how I thank you for
my skill."

The reader is reminded of "A une Madone" in *Les Fleurs du mal,* but
whereas the verse poem is marked by a passion whose violence verges on
hysteria, the prose poem reveals a highly controlled emotion that is as coldly
ironical as it is cruel. In certain respects the poem is more reminiscent of
"Une Charogne," for in it is to be found the same note of irritation, the same
irony, the same exaggerated courtesy, and even the same admission of the
inspiration she—"his inevitable and pitiless Muse"—awakened in him.

The macabre note found in "Le Galant Tireur" is even more obvious in
"Les Tentations" and in "Mademoiselle Bistouri," in both of which the poet
explores the relationship of love and violence. In "Les Tentations" Eros wears
a live serpent as a belt that is hung with sinister phials and surgical instruments. The germ of the poem seems to be an idea Baudelaire had already
expressed in *Fusées:* "In the act of love, there is a striking resemblance to torture or to a surgical operation" (*OC,* 1:659). Elsewhere in his *Journaux intimes* Baudelaire describes the act of love as something criminal—"a crime
which necessitates an accomplice" (*OC,* 1:689).

The feeling of incommunicability and incompatibility that marked
Baudelaire's relationship with all women, save the old, the decrepit, and the
rejected is again emphasized in "La Soupe et les nuages," in which the poet-
aesthete is roused from his contemplation of the moving clouds by a heavy

blow on his back and is brought back to reality by the "raucous and charming" voice of his mistress, who orders the "damnable old cloud merchant" to go and eat his supper.

"Portraits de maîtresses" provided Baudelaire an opportunity not only to depict the various types of women he had known but also to reveal, through the conversation of four dandies, certain aspects of his own personality. The discussion of three of the gentlemen regarding their respective mistresses is based not on physical love, but rather on infidelity, incompatibility, and greed, all of which are obviously inspired by Jeanne.

Somewhat surprising, however, is the admission of the fourth gentleman that his former mistress' greatest fault was a perfection so great that he found himself admiring—but "with a heart full of hate"—her lack of those foibles that mark the human condition and that cause us to seek an ideal that seems unattainable.

We are reminded of his statement in *Le Salon de 1846:* "Poets, artists, and the whole human race would be very unhappy, if the ideal, that absurdity, that impossibility were found. What would each one do hereafter with his *"pauvre moi?"* (*OC*, 2:455).

"Portraits de maîtresses" is in striking contrast to "Un Cheval de race" (1864) in which Baudelaire is obviously paying homage to Jeanne, although she remains unnamed. To the poet she is still "délicieuse," "exquise," and "héroïque" despite the fact that age has made her ugly, decrepit, and skeletonlike in appearance. Moreover, time has failed to destroy either her graceful walk or the indestructible elegance of her figure that Baudelaire had long since celebrated in "Le Serpent qui danse" of *Les Fleurs du mal*. Although the description itself is made deliberately prosaic and surprising in its contradictory comparisons, the form and structure retain an element of the poetic, derived as it is from a pattern calculated to suggest the stanzas and even at times the refrain of a lyric poem.

An example of the genuine compassion that Baudelaire felt for Jeanne and for older women in general, "Un Cheval de race" stands in striking contrast to the aversion he felt for the young girl secure in her youth and beauty. We have only to remember his comment in *Mon Coeur mis à nu:* "A little fool and a little slut; the greatest stupidity joined to the greatest depravity. There is in the young girl all the degradation of the guttersnipe and the schoolgirl" (*OC*, 1:698).

Among the finest of Baudelaire's longer prose poems—in reality a short story that recalls Poe's *Imp of the Perverse*—is "Le Mauvais Vitrier." Summoned to the sixth-floor garret of a poet, who had heard his piercing cries calling his wares, a glazier laboriously climbs the six flights, carrying with him his precious panes of glass.

Failing to find among the lot any colored panes that would enable him to see "la vie en beau," the poet angrily dismisses the poor man, who slowly and with great difficulty, descends the stairs. On reaching the street, the glazier meets with further disaster: the poet hurls down on him a pot of flowers, smashes all the glass panes that represented the poor man's earnings for the day, and, as if "intoxicated by his fit of madness," cries out, "la vie en beau! la vie en beau!" The poet's cry mitigates in part the sadistic cruelty of his act, for it reveals his deep disappointment in life and his desperate need to transform the ugliness of reality into something more beautiful. Acknowledging the danger of his excitable act, the poet-narrator concludes: "But what matters the eternity of damnation to one who has found in a second an infinity of joy?"

There seems every reason to believe that the incident recounted by Baudelaire is also related to his belief in an Evil Spirit, or as he states in the opening paragraph, to a "mysterious and unexplained impulse" that causes "natures which are purely contemplative and wholly unfit for action" to perform "the most absurd and often the most dangerous of actions." Neither the moralist nor the doctor, he adds, can explain "so mad an energy (that) is suddenly aroused in these idle and voluptuous souls."

We are reminded of Baudelaire's reply on 26 June 1860 to a letter that had been sent him by Flaubert, in which the novelist had chided the poet for insisting "a little too much" on the presence of an Evil Spirit in *Les Paradis Artificiels*. "I have always been obsessed," Baudelaire replied, "by the impossibility of accounting for some of man's *sudden acts and thoughts* except by the hypothesis of the intervention of an *evil force outside himself*" [italics added] (*Corr.*, 1:53). In "Le Mauvais Vitrier," Baudelaire makes a somewhat similar observation in describing a particular state of mind that, as he maintains, "doctors call hysterical, and people more thoughtful than doctors call Satanic"—a state of mind which impels man to commit many dangerous or improper actions without offering any resistance. Baudelaire himself had experienced, it seems, a somewhat similar state of mind, as he suggests in a letter to his mother on 26 March 1853: "Why, though I have a true and clear idea of duty and practicality, do I always do the opposite?" (*Corr.*, 1:214). And in his *Fusées*, he observes that both man and woman know from birth that in evil may be found "toute volupté" (*OC*, 1:652).

It is interesting to note, as Lemaitre points out, that the urban context is not a simple décor in this case, but another example of the poet's tendency to associate satanic perversity with the foul and heavy atmosphere of an urban setting, such as is found in his famous poem, "Le Crépuscule du soir."[12]

Like "Le Mauvais Vitrier," "Mademoiselle Bistouri" is likewise characteristic of Poe, particularly in its length and in its prosaic qualities. In the streets of Paris, the poet encounters a strange creature whose mental derangement becomes more and more obvious as the story progresses. In her stubborn conviction that the poet is a doctor, she insists that he accompany her to her home where her conversation reveals not only a bizarre obsession with the macabre—in this case the surgical instruments and the bloody apron of a surgeon—but also a gentleness and sensitivity to the plight of others that surprises her guest as much as it does the reader.

The story ends with a prayer in which Baudelaire, questioning God's motives and, indirectly, his goodness, begs for his pity on all those who are afflicted by madness. His preoccupation with the question of insanity may well have been inspired by certain events in his own life. He must surely have remembered the kind and gentle Nerval, whose fits of insanity finally led to his tragic suicide, as well as the gifted artist Méryon whose sadomasochistic behavior, similar to that of Mlle Bistouri, led to his incarceration in the insane asylum at Charenton, where he finally died from self-imposed starvation. Moreover, Baudelaire himself suffered from the fear of losing his own mind, as we know from the pathetic notation found in his *Journaux intimes:* "I have cultivated my hysteria with joy and terror. Now I am always dizzy, and today 23 January 1862, I experienced a strange warning; I felt passing over me *the wind of the wing of madness*" (*OC*, 1:668).

"It would perhaps be pleasant to be alternately victim and executioner," Baudelaire once wrote in his journal—a whim that he succeeded in carrying out vicariously in "Une Mort heroïque," perhaps the most successful and brilliant of his prose poems. In length and in its use of atmosphere and narration, the story resembles one of Poe's tales, although the plot was borrowed from a work of Brierre de Boismont that Baudelaire is known to have read.[13]

For the actor Nourrit, who serves as the protagonist in Boismont's story, "a partial success was the beginning of his ills, and a hiss that he believed to have heard was a death sentence." This is precisely the motivation used by the poet to explain the sudden death of Fancioulle. A loud, prolonged hiss, instigated by the prince and performed at his request by a small boy, proved to be so devastating a shock that he stopped short, tottered, and fell dead on the floor of the stage.

It is in his analysis and portrayal of character rather than in the plot itself that Baudelaire excels; he reveals a keen understanding of the complex
elements of his own personality with which he endows each of the two
protagonists. Fancioulle, the mime, who had entered a plot against the
despotic prince is not, as is sometimes claimed, the childish revolutionary
that was Baudelaire early in 1848, but rather Baudelaire the serious disci-
ple of Proudhon, who not only had warned the socialist reformer of a plot
against his life, but had also offered him his own assistance and that of his
friends.

In fact, the opening paragraphs of the story are in reality a description of
Baudelaire's state of mind at that very period in his past: "For a person pro-
fessionally devoted to the comic [substitute "the arts"], serious matters have
a fatal attraction and, though it may seem strange that ideas of patriotism
and liberty should despotically take possession of an actor's [substitute
"writer's"] brain—one day Fancioulle joined a conspiracy formed by some
discontented nobles."

Moreover, "the indestructable halo" around the clown's head—invisible
to all but the narrator—"that mingled in a strange amalgam the rays of Art
and the glory of the Martyr" look back to "the mystic crown" and to the
"pure light and primitive rays" to which Baudelaire had referred in his poem
"Bénédiction." Equally characteristic of Baudelaire's thought is Fancioulle's
ability to demonstrate through his brilliant acting that Art is more able than
all else in life "to veil the terror of the tomb."

In the prince, the reader recognizes Baudelaire's "excessive sensibility," his
"passionate love of the arts," his "excellence as a connoisseur," his "insatiable
delight in pleasure," and above all his knowledge that "no enemy is more
dangerous than the feeling of ennui." It is the combination of the last two
traits—his love of pleasure and his fear of ennui—that remind us not only
of the poet in "Le Mauvais Vitrier," but also of a notation expressed by
Baudelaire in his *Journaux intimes:* "Cruelty and 'volupté,' identical sensations, like extreme heat and extreme cold" (*OC,* 1:683).

To the narrator, however, it seemed even more probable that the prince
was chiefly motivated by his desire to perform "a physiological experiment
of a *capital* interest and to verify to what extent the habitual faculties of an
artist could be altered or modified by the extraordinary situation in which
he found himself." In real life, Baudelaire had evinced some of this same intellectual curiosity, as we have already noted, in his wish to be alternately
victim and executioner. In the case of the prince, it is obviously the desire to
play the part of the executioner—a wish prompted in part by jealousy as
well as by curiosity.

The story concludes with the mental cogitations of Baudelaire the narrator who, with seemingly deceptive irony, answers the questions that arise in his own mind. To the query of whether or not the prince had suspected the "homicidal efficacy of his ruse," he answers simply: "It is permissible to doubt it." And to the problem of whether or not the prince would miss his "dear and inimitable Fancioulle," he replies with equal equanimity: "It is nice and legitimate to think so." Earlier in the story, the narrator had wondered whether or not the prince had any intention of offering clemency to the conspirators. And to his own question he had given a tantalizing answer: "That is a point that has never been clarified."

It would seem that in "La Mort héroïque" Baudelaire is deliberately leaving "a lacuna that is to be filled by the imagination"—a lacuna which he had claimed in his essay on Wagner is to be found "even in literature—the most concrete of all the arts" (*OC*, 2:781–82). As he had written in his essay on *Madame Bovary*, "It is for the reader to draw his conclusions from the conclusion" (*OC*, 2:81–82).

"La Corde," another of the short stories reminiscent of Poe, recounts the actual suicide of Manet's charming young helper Alexandre. The child of an indigent family, Alexandre, despite a mischievous air, was subject to strange fits of melancholy for which the narrator offers no explanation. Alexandre's only fault seemed to be his frequent thefts of sugar and liqueurs despite the artist's protests and his threats to return the child to his family.

On returning home one day, Manet discovered to his horror that the boy had committed suicide by hanging himself with a rope attached to a nail above the door. On being told the tragic news, the mother showed no signs of emotion, asking only to be given the rope by which the boy had hanged himself.

What the artist had originally thought to be an expression of maternal love and grief he later discovered was merely a matter of greed—the wish to acquire money by selling portions of the rope to those superstitious enough to believe that such an acquisition would bring good luck. Nowhere has Baudelaire shown himself more ironic in the depiction of maternal love.

The fits of melancholy to which the child was prone seem to be one of the most important clues to the suicide. Again it is tempting to associate the cause of suicide with Baudelaire's own moments of despair, as well as with his own halfhearted attempt to commit suicide as a young man. Moreover, Baudelaire must surely have had in mind the melancholia of his friend Nerval, who finally ended his life by hanging himself from a lamp post in a dark and obscure alley.

There is a tendency to denigrate the aesthetic value of *Le Spleen de Paris* as compared to *Les Fleurs du mal*. It is certainly true that, unlike *Les Fleurs du mal* or even the poetic passages in Chateaubriand and certain other prose writers of the nineteenth century, they are lacking in most of the qualities that we associate with verse. In fact, we are often left with the impression that at times Baudelaire is deliberately avoiding poetic techniques and is attempting to adopt a style that, in its stress on the prosaic, comes close to that used by Poe in his short stories.

Moreover, the heterogeneous nature of both subject and style inevitably increased the difficulty of finding an all-encompassing title for this collection. Many, if not most, of the prose poems show no formal resemblance to verse except in their density. Some are conversations, dialogues, or dreams; others, like "Les Bon Chiens" and "Les Veuves" come closer to an essay in their use of digressions; still others, like "Mademoiselle Bistouri" and "Une Mort célèbre," are actually short stories marked by a simplicity and an economy of means characteristic of Poe. Baudelaire evidently found that through the use of prose, he was able to give greater realism, truth, and immediacy to the ideas that came to preoccupy him more and more and, in so doing, to utilize such tones as irony, sarcasm, and what André Breton has called "black humor." There seems every reason to believe that his use of conversation between the travelers and the nontravelers in "Le Voyage" may have helped him realize the possibility of expanding that technique even further and of basing an entire prose poem, "L'Etranger," on a series of questions and answers. Nor should it be forgotten that Baudelaire himself admitted to Sainte-Beuve's secretary Troubat that the prose poems were in reality an extension of *Tableaux parisiens* but with greater emphasis on "liberté, détail, and raillerie."

From even our casual examination of a few of the most typical prose poems it soon becomes obvious that it is not the real world with which Baudelaire is concerned, but rather a fusion of the real and the imaginary. With but few exceptions, he has succeeded in discovering and portraying those elements of the "marvelous" that, as he wrote in *Le Salon de 1846,* envelop us like the atmosphere itself—almost always those elements of the marvelous that emphasize the ugly and the cruel.

Moreover, his preoccupation with the idea of original sin seems even more obvious than in his earlier writings, and the postulation of sin and vice almost completely outweighs the postulation of the spiritual and the ideal. The result is a universe that is predominately violent, even surreal. It is not man's "grandeur," but his "misère," that the poet celebrates. Even worse, it is

his cruelty, his savagery, his violence, his inability to escape his earthly confines, to "soar above the life below . . . and to understand the language of
flowers and of mute things." There is nothing comparable to the peace and
serene beauty of "Harmonie du soir," "Recueillement," or "Un Balcon"—
nothing that touches the heart as in "Le Cygne" or "La Servante au bon
coeur."

If the ideal exists in the prose poems it leads only to spleen, and the
reader is left with a sense of a universe that is full of chaos, violence, and
moral anarchy. Nor could it be otherwise, given the poet's intention, as he
had stated in his letter to Sainte-Beuve in 1866, to point out "une morale
désagréable" (*Corr.*, 2:583). Moreover, there is prevalent in many of the
prose poems a note of crude savagery, of man's inhumanity to man. True, a
note of cruelty and sadism is also present in certain poems of *Les Fleurs du
mal*, but it is the more refined sadism of "A une Madone" compared to that
of "La Femme sauvage," who devours live chickens and rabbits before the
gaping crowd.

The poet himself is no longer the "seer" or the sacred figure of the Romanticists. Nor is he the albatross, magnificent in flight but clumsy and ridiculous on earth. Like all humanity, he is utterly lacking in the "grandeur"
that compensates for his "misère." Or, as Baudelaire suggests in the more
prosaic style of his prose poem, the poet has lost his halo in the mire of the
street and makes no effort to regain his loss.

Often the poet associates himself with the fool or the clown, revealing the
same hopelessness and sense of rejection that characterize the clown portrayed by Daumier. Nor are the other characters representing the contradictory elements of his fragmented personality any more admirable. In the
individual poems of *Les Fleurs du mal*, Baudelaire had usually represented
only one side of his nature; in the prose poems characters become more
complex as a result of his tendency to attribute contradictory elements of his
own personality to several characters.

Women are no longer idealized, as was sometimes true in *Les Fleurs du
mal*, but are all made to appear selfish, vulgar, and cruel—with the exception of the widow or the older woman, for whom he seems to feel both
tenderness and compassion. In his attitude toward them, Baudelaire was
either influenced by thoughts of his own mother and his kindly old friend
Mme Meurice, or may simply have associated them with the rejected and
the outcasts of society—in other words, with himself. Obviously it was
Baudelaire himself who had need of the "rose-colored panes" that the poet
demanded of the glazier in "Le Mauvais Vitrier," for in the prose poems,
with the exception of "Le Thyrse" and "Les Bons Chiens," he saw only the

stupidity, the cruelty, the injustice, and the utter bleakness of the world around him.

The prose poem usually begins abruptly with little or no introduction, and the reader is plunged immediately and without preparation into the story, as in "Une Mort Héroïque": "Fancioulle was an admirable clown, and almost one of the friends of the Prince." Others begin with a question, as in "Les Yeux des pauvres": "Ah, you want to know why I hate you today." Still others begin with a maxim that he either invents himself or in which he makes certain slight changes. "Anywhere Out of This World" begins with the provocative statement, "This life is a hospital in which each patient is possessed by the wish to change beds." The title was borrowed from Ralph Waldo Emerson, with whose works Baudelaire was acquainted.[14] In the last chapter of his *Conduct of Life,* Emerson had written: "Like sick men in hospitals, we change only from bed to bed." In "Anywhere out of this Life," Baudelaire consciously or unconsciously, alters the wording, producing a more dramatic and effective result.

It is only in the prose versions based on poems found in *Les Fleurs du mal,* such as "La Belle Dorothée" or "Le Crépuscule du soir," that Baudelaire is almost obliged to retain the descriptive passages with which the prose poems begin, since the verse poems were almost entirely descriptive.

Commensurate with the gloomy picture he paints of his fellow-beings, Baudelaire has chosen a style that is marked by irony, bitterness, and "black humor." Gone is the "sorcellerie évocatrice" or the "suggestive magic" of *Les Fleurs du mal.* Instead we have the "ton raisonneur"—an appeal to reason rather than to the emotions—and the use of narration and exposition.

While there is a suggestion of what Hiddleston calls "a quasi-stanzaic structure" in the earlier prose poems, it soon gives way to a deliberately prosaic style that appeals more to the intellect than to the emotions.[15] Among the most striking characteristics of the *Spleen de Paris* is the loss of the musical and suggestive qualities that mark *Les Fleurs du mal* and a greater emphasis on narration, exposition, and a preoccupation with ideas.

The bad luck (*guignon*) to which Baudelaire had attributed Poe's misfortunes was to haunt him as well in his new venture. The public was apathetic—so much so that the publication of a series of prose poems in the *Figaro* was interrupted during 1864 "simply because my poems were boring everyone," as Baudelaire wrote to his mother (*Corr.,* 2:159).

There were times when Baudelaire was too ill to meet his commitments or when journals that had accepted his offerings were forced to cease publi-

cation. There were constant quarrels with editors and publishers who objected to certain poems or to wordings they considered unpublishable.

It was only after the poet's death that, through the efforts of Asselineau
and Banville, the volume of fifty poems was finally published in 1869.
Only then did the reading public first begin to recognize the originality and
the remarkable literary merit of the prose poems and to discover among
them certain "jewels," the term Sainte-Beuve used to describe "Le Vieux
Saltimbanque" and "Les Veuves."[16]

Conclusion

A half century was to pass after Baudelaire's death before the literary world came to realize that he was not merely "a talented poet," but that he was truly "a man of genius," as Banville had affirmed in speaking over the poet's grave in the cemetery of Montparnasse.

Moreover, Baudelaire's criticism—whether on art, literature, or music—remains as pertinent and fascinating today as when it was first written. As Jonathan Mayne has so well observed in the introduction to his *Art in Paris* (1845–62), published by the Phaidon Press in 1965: "He [Baudelaire] may have been a literary and social monster, as he probably was; but borrower, pilferer, even plagiarist (by demonstration) he paradoxically remains one of the great originals of the nineteenth century."

Once Baudelaire's works became public property in 1917, editions soon began to multiply. In 1922 Jacques Crépet, following in his father's footsteps and aided by Claude Pichois, undertook the monumental critical edition of Baudelaire's complete works that was published by Conard. Comprising nineteen volumes, it was produced between 1922 and 1953 and has proved an invaluable tool for Baudelairean scholars.

Of the critical editions that have appeared since that time, none has equaled the superb scholarship demonstrated by Claude Pichois in his own four-volume *Pléiade* critical edition, consisting of two volumes devoted to Baudelaire's correspondence and another two volumes containing his complete works.

Baudelaire's influence on future poets has been enormous. His immediate successors, Verlaine, Mallarmé, and Rimbaud, each found in him a point of departure. For still others, including the Symbolists, he extended the frontiers of poetry by opening up new paths. Today his genius is universally recognized, and his works, as the late W. T. Bandy demonstrated, have been translated into more languages than any other book save the Bible.

Notes and References

Chapter One

1. *Oeuvres complètes*, 2 vols., ed. C. Pichois (Paris: Gallimard, 1975), 1:703; hereafter cited in text as *OC*.

2. It would seem that even as a child Baudelaire experienced what he later was to describe as "spleen." Later in life (30 December 1857) in a letter to his mother Baudelaire described his own "spleen" as "an immense discouragement, an unbearable sensation of loneliness, a perpetual fear of some vague misfortune, a complete lack of confidence in my powers, a total absence of desires, the impossibility of finding anything to distract my mind."

3. *Correspondance*, 2 vols., ed. C. Pichois (Paris: Gallimard, 1973), 439; hereafter cited in text as *Corr.*

4. Jean Ziegler, "Emil Deroy et l'Esthétique de Baudelaire," *Gazette des Beaux-Arts*, May–June, 1976: 153–60.

5. W. T. Bandy, "La Vérité sur *Le Jeune Enchanteur, Baudelaire and Croly*," *Mercure de France*, February, 1950: 233–47.

6. Eugène Crépet, *Baudelaire: Etude biographique*, revised and completed by Jacques Crépet (Paris: Messein, 1907), 79.

7. Marcel Ruff, *Etudes baudelairiennes*, vol. 3 (Neuchatel: Baconnière, 1973), 212.

8. See *The Journal of Eugène Delacroix*, trans. Walter Pach (New York: Covici, Friede, 1937), 182–83: "M. Baudelaire came in as I was starting to work anew. . . . He ran on to Proudhon whom he admires and whom he calls the idol of the people."

9. Gerstle Mack, *Gustave Courbet* (New York: Knopf, 1951), 70.

10. W. T. Bandy, "New Light on Baudelaire and Poe," *Yale French Studies*, no. 10 (Fall–Winter 1952): 65–69.

11. Ibid.

12. Jacques Crépet, *Baudelaire: "Les Fleurs du mal"* (Paris: Conard), 316.

13. Crépet, *Baudelaire. Etudes Biographique*, 124.

14. Ibid., 124.

15. Adolphe Tabarant, *Manet et ses oeuvres* (Paris: Gallimard, 1913), 132.

16. Lois Boe Hyslop and Francis Hyslop, "Baudelaire and Manet: A Re-Appraisal" in *Baudelaire as a Love Poet and Other Essays*, ed. Lois Boe Hyslop (University Park: Pennsylvania State University Press, 1969), 87–130.

17. Claude Pichois, *Etudes Baudelairiennes*, vols. 4–5, *Lettres à Baudelaire* (Neuchatel: Baconnière, 1973), 155.

18. Ibid., 347.

19. *Baudelaire et Asselineau,* texts collected and commented on by Jacques Crépet and Claude Pichois (Paris: Nizet 1953), 252.

20. Marcel Ruff, *Baudelaire, L'Homme et l'oeuvre* (Paris: Hatier-Boivin 1955), 193.

Chapter Two

1. Haussoullier's painting was lost until 1937. It was not shown again until 1969 at the Petit Palais in Paris.

2. This is reminiscent of Zola's definition of a work of art which, he maintained, "is a corner of nature seen through a temperament."

3. During the few short years that Baudelaire was imbued with the socialist and democratic ideas that inspired the Revolution of 1848 and that were being preached by Proudhon and other social reformers, he adopted a philosophy of action that he especially advocated in his essay on Pierre Dupont.

4. It should be noted, however, that Méryon suffered from bouts of insanity, whereas Baudelaire was inspired by the power of his imagination.

5. See letter to Louis Martinet, July 1861 *(Corr., 2: 176).*

6. Nils Sandblat, *Manet, Three Studies in Artistic Conception* (Lund: C. W. K. Gleerup, 1954), 32.

7. In the case of Mallarmé, however, it is not simply a "lacuna" but the entire poem whose mysterious meaning must be discovered by the reader.

8. Mario Praz, *The Romantic Agony* (New York: Meridian Books 1956), 56.

9. Lloyd Austin, *L'Univers poétique de Baudelaire* (Paris: Mercure de France 1956), 29.

10. Robert Vivier, *L'Originalité de Baudelaire* (Brussels: Académie Royale 1965), 298.

11. On a visit to Paris in 1862, Swinburne had picked up a copy of *Les Fleurs du mal* and was so impressed by its beauty that he wrote an anonymous review for the *Spectator.* Though Swinburne had enthusiastically praised the color and perfume of Baudelaire's verse, his perfect workmanship, and his sensuous and weighty style, he had objected to its "distinct and vivid background of morality."

Despite the fact that he sent Baudelaire a copy of the review accompanied by a letter, he was not to receive an answer. The reason was discovered many years later. Baudelaire had indeed replied to Swinburne's letter. Unfortunately, he gave it to Nadar to deliver in person during a trip to London. Nadar absentmindedly put the letter in his briefcase and only discovered it forty years later, three years after the death of Swinburne.

In 1866, on hearing a false rumor of Baudelaire's death, Swinburne wrote "Ave Atque Vale," which he dedicated to the French poet.

12. Crépet, *Baudelaire: "Les Fleurs du mal,"* 373–74.

Chapter Three

1. Jacques Crépet, *Propos sur Baudelaire,* collected and annotated by Claude Pichois (Paris: Mercure de France, 1957), 46.

2. Charles Baudelaire, *Journaux intimes,* ed. Jacques Crépet and Georges Blin (Paris: 1949), 303. See also Margaret Gilman, *Baudelaire the Critic* (New York: 1943), 191–93.

3. Lois Boe Hyslop, "Baudelaire on *Les Misérables,*" *French Review* 41, no. 1 (October 1967): 23–29.

4. Asselineau's comment on *Les Misérables* confirms Baudelaire's dislike of the novel: "Certainly he admired Victor Hugo. He has admitted it publicly in many an article, especially in his review contained in the *Poètes français* of E. Crépet. In order to correct certain falsehoods, he even insisted on publishing in a journal a review of *Les Misérables* in which he revealed all his dexterity; for, at heart, the book with its moral outrageousness, its leaden paradoxes, deeply irritated him." See Chapter 1, note 16.

5. Baudelaire's admission to his mother that he *knew how to "lie"*—a claim that he obviously made in a moment of bravado—was not as exaggerated as it might seem. Critics, and even Hugo himself, have seemed unaware of what at best might be labeled casuistry, if not duplicity.

6. It is true that Banville was one of those at whom Baudelaire scoffed in his essay "L'Ecole païenne," but elsewhere, both in his correspondence and in his literary criticism, the poet-critic speaks of him with only the highest praise.

7. Claude Pichois, *Lettres à Baudelaire,* 153.

8. Lois Boe Hyslop, "Baudelaire: "Madame Bovary, c'est moi," *Kentucky Romance Quarterly* 20, no. 3 (1973).

9. *Baudelaire et Asselineau,* 19.

10. Georges Poulet, *Etude sur le temps humain* (Paris: Plon, 1950), 305.

Chapter Four

1. In the essay itself we note such similarities as: "I felt as if I were being lifted up above the earth." . . . "I felt myself freed from the *bonds of weight,* and in memory I recaptured the extraordinary *pleasure* which floats about heights." . . . "I fully conceived the idea of a soul moving in a luminous milieu, of an ecstacy *composed of pleasure and knowledge* and soaring far beyond the natural world" (*OC,* 2:784, 785).

It should also be noted that in a letter to Wagner (17 February 1860), Baudelaire describes his sensation on listening to the music as one of "rising into the air and of rolling on the sea." *Corr.,* 2:675.

2. Lois Boe Hyslop, "Baudelaire's *Elévation* and E. T. A. Hoffmann," *French Review,* Vol. 45, no. 5 (April 1973): 951–59.

3. Austin, *L'Univers Poétique de Baudelaire,* 195.

4. Alison Fairlie, *Les Fleurs du mal* (London: Edward Arnold Ltd. 1960), 36.

5. Lois Boe Hyslop, "Baudelaire's *Hymne à la Beauté*," *Nineteenth-Century French Studies* 7, nos. 3/4, (Spring–Summer 1979): 202–12.

6. A great admirer of Baudelaire, Proust was fascinated by the relationship of his own conception of memory to that of the poet: "In the case of Baudelaire . . . it is the poet himself who, with more deliberation . . . voluntarily seeks in the scent of a woman's hair or breast the stimulating analogies that will evoke for him 'the azure of the immense, encircling sky' and 'a port filled with masts and pennants.'" See Marcel Proust, *Le Temps retrouvé* (Paris: Gallimard, 1949), 73.

Elsewhere (in *Contre Sainte-Beuve*), Proust calls Baudelaire "the greatest poet of the nineteenth century" and criticizes Sainte-Beuve for failing to recognize the quality of imagination in *Les Fleurs du mal*.

7. See Erich Auerbach, "The Aesthetic Dignity of the *Fleurs du mal*" in *Baudelaire, A Collection of Critical Essays,* ed. by Henri Peyre (Englewood Cliffs, N.J.: Prentice-Hall, 1962), 168.

8. Baudelaire, *Les Fleurs du mal,* with introduction and notes by Antoine Adam (Paris: Garnier frères, 1961), 361.

9. Ibid., 368.

10. Baudelaire, *Les Fleurs du mal,* critical edition by Jacques Crépet et Georges Blin (Paris, 1942), p. 261, n. 3.

11. *Les Fleurs du mal,* ed. Antoine Adam 383.

12. See *OC,* 1:445: "You haven't noticed that in *Les Fleurs du mal* there are two poems concerning you or at least alluding to intimate details of our former life, going back to that time of your widowhood and sad memories."

13. P. Mansell Jones, *Baudelaire,* Studies in Modern European Literature (New Haven, Conn.: Yale University Press, 1952), 49–50.

14. *Les Fleurs du mal,* ed. Adam, 398.

15. Ibid., 408.

16. Jean Prévost, *Baudelaire, Essai sur l'inspiration et la Création Poetique* (Paris: Mercure de France, 1953), 240.

17. Vivier, *L'Originalité de Baudelaire,* 31.

18. Hyslop, "Baudelaire, Proudhon, and Le Reniement de Saint-Pierre," 273–286.

19. P. J. Proudhon, *Carnets* (Paris: Marcel Rivières, 1961), 2:272.

20. Ibid., 272.

21. M. Riffaterre, "L'Etude stylistique des formes littéraires conventionelles." *French Review,* XXXVIII (October 1964), 3–14. [A defense of the second stanza of "Recueillement," against Valéry's criticism in particular.]

Chapter Five

1. *Revue de Paris,* 15 April 1921: *Charles Baudelaire, à propos de Centenaire,* 727.

2. Charles Baudelaire, *Petits Poèmes en prose,* Introduction, Notes, Bibliography and Selections by Henri Lemaître (Paris: Garnier, 1958), 22.

3. In "Le Poème du hachisch," Baudelaire defines *rhapsodic* as "a train of thoughts suggested and ordered by the exterior world and by chance circumstances."

4. Suzanne Bernard, *Le Poème en prose de Baudelaire jusqu'à nos jours* (Paris: Nizet, 1959) 147, [my translation].

5. J. A. Hiddleston, *Baudelaire et Le Spleen de Paris* (Oxford: The Clarendon Press, 1987), 29.

6. Now in the National Gallery, Washington, D.C. In Daumier's drawing, however, both woman and child appear placid and serene.

7. Hyslop, "Baudelaire and Manet: A Re-appraisal" 87–130.

8. The germ of the story may be found in a notation that appears in the *Journaux intimes:* "When a man gets into the habit of laziness, of day-dreaming, of complete idleness to the extent of postponing something important until the next day, if another man should wake him in the morning with a whip and beat him mercilessly until, not being able to work with pleasure, the latter worked out of fear, wouldn't that man with the whip be his true friend, his benefactor?" *OC,* 1:655.

9. Baudelaire was deeply impressed by the ideas of Joseph de Maistre as well as those of Poe.

10. The lyricism of the opening paragraphs is in reality a pastiche of Lamartine's poem "Le Vallon."

11. That Baudelaire had read Proudhon's *Philosophie de la misère* is well known. He had even copied passages from the volume into his notebook.

12. Henri Lemaitre, *Charles Baudelaire: Petits Poèmes en Prose* (Paris: Garnier 1958), 43, n.1.

13. Both Jacques Crépet and Robert Kopp agree that the idea of the sudden death of Fancioulle was obviously suggested by a similar incident recounted in a book by Boismont that Baudelaire is known to have read. See Kopp, *Petits Poèmes en Prose* (Paris: Corti, 1969), 290; Crépet, *Petits Poèmes en Prose* (Paris, Conard, 1926), 316.

14. See Margaret Gilman, "Baudelaire and Emerson," *Romantic Review* (October 1943): 222. See also Kopp, *Petits Poèmes en Prose* 351.

15. Hiddleston, *Baudelaire et Le Spleen de Paris,* 80–81.

16. Marcel Ruff, *Baudelaire,* tr. and slightly abridged by Agnes Kertesz (New York: New York University Press, 1966), 159.

Selected Bibliography

PRIMARY WORKS

Oeuvres complètes, 19 vols., ed. Jacques Crépet and Claude Pichois (last 3 vols.). Paris: Conard, 1922–53.

Oeuvres complètes, 2 vols., ed. Claude Pichois. Paris: Gallimard, 1975.

Correspondance, 2 vols., ed. Claude Pichois. Paris: Gallimard, 1973.

Petits Poëmes en Prose. Critical Edition by Robert Kopp. Paris: José Corti, 1969. A definitive study of Baudelaire's prose poems, containing a preface, introduction, the 1869 text (with variants), notes, commentaries, and bibliography.

The Painter of Modern Life and Other Essays. Translated and edited by Jonathan Mayne. London: Phaidon, 1964. Contains Baudelaire's famous essay on Constantin Guys, in whom the critic discovered the painter of modern life. The volume also contains important studies of Delacroix, Poe, and Wagner, as well as more general studies on subjects such as caricature and on what Baudelaire scornfully termed "philosophic art." Notes on the illustrations are included in the final section. The translation is both accurate and brilliant.

Art in Paris, 1845–1862, Reviews of Salons and Other Exhibitions. Translated and edited by Jonathan Mayne. London: Phaidon, 1965. Together with its companion-volume, *The Painter of Modern Life,* it reveals Baudelaire's astute knowledge of the visual arts of his time. Notes on the illustrations are included in a final section of the volume.

The Flowers of Evil. Selected and edited by Marthiel and Jackson Mathews. The volume contains not only the original poems in French, but also the translations, chosen from many, by the Mathews. The book includes "Three Drafts of a Preface," taken from the critical edition of *Les Fleurs du mal* by E. Crépet and G. Blin, which were originally intended to serve as prefaces for the 1861 and the 1868 editions of his poems.

The Essence of Laughter and Other Essays, Journals, and Letters. Edited, selected and introduced by Peter Quennell. New York: Meridian Books, 1956. Contains, among other selected works, the entire text of Baudelaire's two journals, *Rockets* and *My Heart Laid Bare,* as well as the complete text of his notebook *Years in Brussels.*

Selected Letters: The Conquest of Solitude. Translated and edited by Rosemary Lloyd. Chicago: The University of Chicago Press, 1986. An excellent translation accompanied by valuable ancillary material: introduction, chronology, bibliography, notes, and index.

SECONDARY WORKS

Books

Asselineau, Charles. *Charles Baudelaire, sa vie et son oeuvre*. Paris: Lemerre, 1869. Reprinted in *Baudelaire et Asselineau*, collected and commented on by Jacques Crépet et Claude Pichois. Paris: Nizet, 1953.

Austin, Lloyd. *L'Univers Poétique de Baudelaire*. Paris: Mercure de France, 1956. Still one of the best discussions of Baudelaire's poetry.

Bandy, W. T. *Baudelaire Judged by His Contemporaries (1845–1867)*. Publications of the Institute of French Studies. New York: Columbia University Press, 1933.

Bandy, W. T. *Charles Baudelaire et Edgar Allan Poe: sa vie et ses ouvrages*. Toronto: University of Toronto Press, 1973. Presents a complete account of the genesis of Baudelaire's 1852 essay on Poe, with supporting evidence proving his plagiarism from articles appearing in the *Southern Literary Messenger*. An important discovery by a leading Baudelaire scholar.

Bernard, Suzanne. *Le Poème en prose de Baudelaire jusqu'à nos jours*. Paris: Nizet, 1959. A scholarly analysis of the prose poems.

Blin, G. *Le Sadisme de Baudelaire*. Paris: Corti, 1948. Contains a chapter on the *Petits Poëmes en prose* and a refutation of Sartre's *Baudelaire*. A valuable study of Baudelaire's art.

Fairlie, Alison. *Baudelaire: Les Fleurs du mal*. London: Edward Arnold Ltd., 1960. A sensitive analysis of Baudelaire's poetry.

Gilman, Margaret. *Baudelaire the Critic*. New York: Columbia University Press, 1943. Still one of the best studies of Baudelaire's criticism.

Hiddleston, J. A. *Baudelaire and Le Spleen de Paris*. Oxford: The Clarendon Press, 1987. Discussion based mainly on the thematic level.

Hyslop, Lois Boe. *Baudelaire, Man of His Time*. New Haven, Conn.: Yale University Press, 1980.

Hyslop, Lois, and Francis E. Hyslop. *Baudelaire: A Self-Portrait*. Oxford: Oxford University Press, 1957. Westport, Conn: Reprint. Greenwood Press, 1979. Translation of selected letters with a running commentary.

Jones, P. Mansell. *Baudelaire*. New Haven, Conn.: Yale University Press, 1952. A concise and useful study of Baudelaire's aesthetic theories.

Leakey, F. W. *Baudelaire and Nature*. New York: Barnes and Noble, 1969. The evolution of Baudelaire's attitude toward external nature.

Lloyd, Rosemary. *Baudelaire's Literary Criticism*. New York: Cambridge University Press, 1981. A well-documented and important study of Baudelaire's literary criticism seen in the light of oppressive contemporary press laws.

Mossop, D. J. *Baudelaire's Tragic Hero*. Oxford: Oxford University Press, 1961. An attempt to explain the duality of *Les Fleurs du mal*, the opposition between his idealism and his "satanism."

Mouquet, G. and **W. T. Bandy.** *Baudelaire en 1848.* Paris: Emile-Paul, 1946. An account of Baudelaire's political activities in 1848.

Peyre, H. *Connaissance de Baudelaire.* Paris: Libraire José Corti, 1951. Especially important for reference and bibliography.

Peyre, Henri, ed. *Baudelaire—A Collection of Critical Essays,* with an introduction by Henri Peyre. Englewood Cliffs, N.J.: Prentice Hall, 1962. Contains eleven important articles written by eminent Baudelaire scholars.

Pichois, Claude. *Baudelaire.* Trans. Graham Robb, with additional research by Jean Ziegler. New York: Viking Penquin, 1989. A slightly abridged version of the French original. The most recent and authoritative biography of Baudelaire by the leading authority on Baudelaire.

Pichois, Claude, and **Vincenette Pichois.** *Lettres à Baudelaire. Etudes Baudelairiennes, vols. 4 and 5.* Neuchatel: Baconnière, 1967.

Prévost, Jean. *Baudelaire. Essai sur l'inspiration et la création poétiques.* 1953. Reprint. Paris: Mercure de France, 1964. A penetrating study of *Les Fleurs du mal.*

Proust, Marcel. "Situation de Baudelaire," reprinted in *Variété II.* Paris: Gallimard, 1930.

Proust, Marcel. "A propos de Baudelaire," *Nouvelle Revue Française,* June, 1921; reprinted in *Chroniques.* Paris: Gallimard, 1927. Sees in Baudelaire a compassionate, human, and "democratic" poet.

Ruff, Marcel. *Baudelaire.* Translated and slightly abridged by Agnes Kertesz. New York: New York University Press, 1966.

Sandblat, Nils. *Manet: Three Studies in Artistic Conception.* Lund: C. W. K. Gleerup, 1954. Excellent.

Sartre, J.-P. *Baudelaire.* Paris: Gallimard, 1947. English edition trans. M. Turnell. New York: New Directions, 1967. An existentialist interpretation of Baudelaire.

Starkie, Enid. *Baudelaire.* 1933. Reprint. London:, 1957. The fullest biography of Baudelaire, but marred by a few factual errors.

Turnell, Martin. *Baudelaire. A Study of His Poetry.* New York: New Directions, 1972. Presents background and discusses prosody, imagery, and structure. Reestablishes poet's claim to originality. Sometimes controversial.

Vivier, Robert. *L'Originalité de Baudelaire.* 1926. Reprint. Brussels: Renaissance de Livre, 1952 and 1965. Still one of the best studies of Baudelaire's style.

Articles

Auerbach, Eric. "The Aesthetic Dignity of the *Fleurs du mal,"* in *Baudelaire—A Collection of Critical Essays,* ed. Henri Peyre. Englewood Cliffs, N.J.: Prentice-Hall, 1962, 149–69. A remarkable and penetrating study of Baudelaire's poetry.

Bandy, W. T. "La Vérité sur *Le Jeune Enchanteur, Baudelaire & Croly."* *Mercure de*

France (February 1950): 237–47. Bandy's discovery of Baudelaire's plagiarism of a story that had been written by an English divine and published in England.

Chambers, Ross. "'Je' dans les *Tableaux Parisiens de Baudelaire*." *Nineteenth-Century French Studies* 7, nos. 1/2 (Fall–Winter 1980–81): 59–69.

Fairlie, Alison. "Some Remarks on Baudelaire's *Poème du Haschisch*," in *The French Mind*. Oxford: The Clarendon Press, 1952, 291–317. An important and perceptive study.

Heck, Francis S. "'La Beauté': Enigma or Irony." *French Review* 49, no. 3 (February 1976), 328–36. An interesting interpretation of a controversial and much discussed poem.

Heck, Francis S. "'Le Mauvais Vitrier': A Literary Transfiguration." *Nineteenth-Century French Studies* 14, nos. 3/4 (Spring–Summer 1986: 260–67. An excellent interpretation of a much discussed prose poem.

Hyslop, Lois Boe. "Baudelaire on *Les Misérables*." *French Review* 41, no. 1 (October 1967): 23–29. Discusses an article by Baudelaire seemingly favorable enough to be published, yet entirely consistent with his own contrary aesthetic and philosophic ideas. A brilliant tour de force on Baudelaire's part.

Hyslop, Lois Boe. "Baudelaire, Proudhon, and 'Le Reniement de Saint Pierre.'" *French Studies* 30, no. 3 (July 1976): 273–86. The influence of Proudhon on Baudelaire.

Hyslop, Lois, and Francis Hyslop. "Baudelaire and Manet: A Re-Appraisal" in *Baudelaire as a Love Poet and Other Essays,* Ed. Lois Boe Hyslop. University Park: Penn State University Press, 1969, 87–130. An account of the close friendship between Baudelaire and Manet and of the poet's influence on the artist.

Ingman, Heather. "Joachim du Bellay and Baudelaire's *Tableaux Parisiens*." *Nineteenth-Century French Studies* 15, no. 4 (Summer 1987): 407–13.

Patty, James. "Baudelaire et Hippolyte Babou," in centenary issue of *Revue d'Histoire Littéraire de la France* devoted to Baudelaire, (April–June 1967): 36–48. A fascinating account of the obscure writer who suggested to Baudelaire the title *Les Fleurs du mal* and wrote the first review after its publication.

Patty, James S. "Baudelaire and Dürer: Avatars of Melancholia." *Symposium* 38, no. 3 (Fall 1984): 36–48. Explores Baudelaire's interest in Dürer.

Bibliographies

Bulletin Baudelairien. Vanderbilt University. Includes a yearly bibliography.

Cargo, Robert T. *Baudelaire Criticism 1950–1967: A Bibliography with Critical Commentary.* Tuscaloosa, Ala: University of Alabama Press, 1968.

Cargo, Robert T. *A Concordance to Baudelaire's Les Fleurs du mal.* Chapel Hill: University of North Carolina Press, 1965.

Index

The Author

Lois Boe Hyslop holds a Ph.D. from the University of Wisconsin. She retired in 1976 as professor emerita of romance languages from Pennsylvania State University where she was professor of French literature and a fellow of the Institute for the Arts and Humanistic Studies. In collaboration with her husband, Francis E. Hyslop, she has published *Baudelaire on Poe* (1952), *Baudelaire: A Self-Portrait* (1957), and *Baudelaire as a Literary Critic* (1964). In 1969 she edited *Baudelaire as a Love Poet and Other Essays*, to which she and her husband contributed an important essay, "Baudelaire and Manet: A Re-Appraisal." In 1980 Yale University published her most recent book, *Baudelaire: Man of His Time*.

The Editor

David O'Connell is professor of foreign languages and chair of the Department of Foreign Languages at Georgia State University. He received his Ph.D. from Princeton University in 1966, where he was a National Woodrow Wilson Fellow, the Bergen Fellow in Romance Languages, and a National Woodrow Wilson Dissertation Fellow. He is the author of *The Teachings of Saint Louis: A Critical Text* (1972), *Les Propos de Saint Louis* (1974), *Louis-Ferdinand Céline* (1976), *The Instructions of Saint Louis: A Critical Text* (1979), and *Michel de Saint Pierre: A Catholic Novelist at the Crossroads* (1990). He is the editor of *Catholic Writers in France since 1945* (1983) and has served as review editor (1977–79) and Managing editor (1987–90) of the *French Review.*